Now Who is Going to Make
My Coffee

Bonnie and Cliff traveling

Bonnie Flood

Trilogy Christian Publishers
A Wholly Owned Subsidary of Trinity Broadcasting Network
2442 Michelle Drive
Tustin, CA 92780

For information, address Trilogy Christian Publishing
Rights Department, 2442 Michelle Drive, Tustin, Ca 92780.
Trilogy Christian Publishing/ TBN and colophon are trademarks of Trinity Broadcasting Network.

For information about special discounts for bulk purchases, please contact Trilogy Christian Publishing.

Manufactured in the United States of America

10 9 8 7 6 5 4 3 2 1

Library of Congress Cataloging-in-Publication Data is available.

ISBN 978-1-64088-557-8 (Hardcover)
ISBN 978-1-64088-568-5 (ebook)

INTRODUCTION

Now who will make my coffee?

I woke up this morning looking for you.

Smelling my coffee, looking for you. The room is dark, no light, looking for you. Where has the time gone? It seems like yesterday I was in your arms, smelling your shaving lotion, holding my coffee. I hug your chair, but it's empty. I dream of yesterday.

Tears fall like buckets of rain, but I smile, remembering who is holding your hand. It was just part of His plan.

Two weeks before my husband passed away, I woke up one night startled. It was as if I heard a voice saying, "You will write a book called *Who is Going to Make My Coffee*." I thought, how could that be? I'm an artist, not a writer. So I put that aside, thinking it was just a dream.

Months after his death, I recalled that dream and realized it was a voice about my future. My desire to write this book became a passion, along with encouragement from my friend, Dr. Wayne Woods. Dr. Woods has also been a widower for three years. His years of psychology helped me to understand some of the stages of my journey. I think we helped each other.

But my morning coffee remains a problem for me. I hadn't made coffee for thirty years. I tried three coffee makers and returned them, saying something was wrong. Finally, through a friend's wisdom, I bought one with the pods. The coffee is okay but not like before. I will survive.

CHAPTER 1

An Unplanned Journey

Our joys as winged dreams do fly
Why then should sorrow last?
Since grief but aggravates thy loss,
Grieve not for what is past.

—Anonymous

The death of a spouse will probably be the most devastating experience an individual will have in their lifetime. We would wish to go together, but that rarely happens. One is left. Life as we know it seems to end with the death of our spouse. It feels as if we have lost part of ourselves, which we have. To our surprise, the world does not end. Others go about their lives as if nothing has changed, while we cringe with unhappiness and dread life alone.

Each person seeks their own path back from the abyss of darkness to find a method of coping and try to find a level of happiness again. There is no right or wrong journey because everyone is different. There are as many paths as there are individuals in despair. Each person mourns differently, and each must seek a way back—their own way and in their own time. Even if a friend has lost a love one and says they know exactly how you feel, they are wrong. No one but you knows how you feel.

Perhaps the hardest emotion to deal with is the loneliness. I have a male friend who told me he was so lonely, the telemarketers hung up on him! Suddenly we are faced with not only continuing our tasks, but we pick up the added tasks our spouse used to do.

There are some common threads I have discovered writing this book. I've written real stories from real people. Some simple things can make a world of difference to a grieving individual—a simple touch on the arm, a card or note, or a phone call.

I have a friend who just returned from a riverboat cruise from New Orleans to Memphis. On this trip, he met a fellow traveler named John. It seemed John had lost his wife the previous year, and this cruise was the last the two of them took together. He wanted to be alone and try to remember everything he could about their trip.

Seating was assigned for the dinner meal but not for lunch. John told his waitress to seat him at a corner table and not seat anyone else with him.

When my friend showed for lunch, of course he did not know any of this. He had a different waitress, and walking through the dining room, she spotted a gentleman sitting by himself. So she asked my friend if he would mind sitting with someone, and he replied it was fine with him.

When he sat down, he noticed a strange look on John's face. But he introduced himself and asked the man where he was from. During the course of the meal, both men revealed their wives had died. At this point, John began talking about his wife, her occupation, hobbies, and places they had traveled together, including this trip.

My friend simply listened. He gave no advice, no preaching, no telling him he knew how he felt (because you don't know, even if something similar has happen to you). However, my friend did throw out a few questions. When John finished talking about how wonderful his wife was, how perfect she was for him, my friend asked, "Do you think you will ever get married again?" This threw John out of his sad comfort zone and put a thought in his mind he could not have dared think about. He stammered then finally said, "Well…Well, I don't know. I guess, whatever the Lord has in mind for me."

After this lunch, every time John saw my friend on the boat, he wanted to talk. When the trip ended, at the airport, John found my friend again, even though they were flying on different airlines. He said he just wanted to shake his hand. Then he said something strange, something to the effect that he felt maybe the Lord had sent my friend to him in his time of deep distress.

"In Rusty Berkus's *To Heal Again*," he stated, "remember, grief will take as long as it takes, and there is no right or wrong way to grieve, there is just your way." Grief is hard to bear. You know you will never be the same again, which is true, but you can be happy again.

Two eagles are sitting on a limb outside their empty nest. The last of their chicks has learned to fly and soared away to their own adventure. The eagles have mated for life. Sometimes they can be seen in the afternoon sky playing,

7

taking a stick from the talons of the other. This afternoon, it is time to hunt and eat. The male flies up and over the mountains to a small river to hunt for fish. The female flies to the forest to find a rabbit or maybe even a raccoon.

From high in the sky with her keen eyesight, she spots a big-eared rabbit. Silent as air, she dives, hitting the unsuspecting jack rabbit hard and sinking her sharp talons into soft flesh. She pins the rodent down with her weight and begins to eat.

Some distant away, a rifle barrel eases out of the brush. An explosion shatters the stillness of the forest. A well-placed bullet tears through the eagle's body. She utters the squeak chirp sound eagles make, pleading for her mate. Even a valley away, he hears her distress call. He soars up and flies for the forest.

The hunter approaches. The eagle plops away from him, still crying. When he reaches for her, she is dead. He puts her legs together and grips the heavy bird with one hand. Through the forest, he can see smoke coming from his cabin.

"You timed that perfectly. Supper is ready." His wife looks somewhat disdainful at him. "What you got there?"

He replies, "Just an old eagle. It was eating a rabbit or something."

She asks why he shot it. He says he doesn't know. It was just an easy shot so he took it. His wife says, "What are you going to do with it? It ain't good for nothing. Can't eat no eagle."

His son speaks, asking if he can have some of the feathers. The hunter tells him to take all he wants but save one for him to put in his hunting cap. He picks up the remains of the bird and throws it out the door for his dogs.

Later, at nightfall, the son asks the hunter what is the strange sound he keeps hearing in the forest. The father tells him it is just the sound of some old eagle, tells him not to worry and go back to sleep.

Deep in the trees, a lone eagle sits on a branch crying, making the same calling sound over and over, but his mate does not answer. Never again will they play in the sky or soar on the thermal convection currents. He does not understand why, but she never returns.

As I ask more questions of widows, I find the treatment of widows and divorced women is not the same. It was quite an eye-opener when I ended my first abusive marriage. I loved to cook and have parties. I was active in tennis and made many friends. After my divorce, they all disappeared. I got a job in a local department store to support myself and three children.

One day, a group of women I used to hang out with came to try on clothes. The dressing room was left with clothes which needed to be placed back on the racks. One lady said they better hang the clothes so they could go to lunch. Another woman said, "Oh, let Bonnie hang them up. That's what she is here for."

I walked away in tears and told myself I would get through even this with my faith. It opened my eyes. I questioned myself. Had I once been like these women? I was determined to be a better person than the people I had been hanging out with. Six months later, I opened my own designer store. These same women shopped in my store, but seemed to respect me more now.

If you have enjoyed a relationship of deep love and respect, that alone is very comforting. When talking to others about their loss, avoid citing personal experiences or saying,

"I know how you feel." You do not know how they feel, even if your loss seems similar. Always remember when you are speaking with the griever, you should be focused on him or her. One of the best ways to help someone who is grieving is to reminisce about the person who has died. You can remind them or remind yourself the length of time mourning has nothing to do with the depth of love felt for the deceased. Each person's grief time is unique to them. Time will not make the pain of loss go away, but it will lessen the pain. Remember some friendships are solid in times of happiness, but tend to wane during times of grief. There is no right or wrong way to grieve, there is just your way. Grief is hard to bear. You know you will never be the same again.

Many individuals make the statement that they would "just like to run away." But they can't or won't. My same male friend wanted to run away as far as he could from the pain and misery. So he did. He left his comfort zone, friends, home, and style of life, traveling thirteen hundred miles to the mountains of New Mexico, where he lived in a tent and worked at a camp for three months. He said the hardest part was the bathroom being a tenth of a mile from his tent. Going to the restroom in the middle of the night with the temperature at the freezing point had a degree of difficulty. Each morning, the clothes stacked at the end of his cot needed to be shaken to rid them of spiders and scorpions before they could be worn. While in New Mexico, he sold his home and had the contents moved to another house he purchased. He returned to a new neighborhood and attempted to start fresh.

CHAPTER 2

I want to start by telling my story. I grew up in a small Amish town in Indiana. At ten years of age, my sister and I became Christians. A school teacher picked the two of us up every Sunday for church. She also drove my sister and me to church camps. I was surrounded with four siblings—Dee, Don, Jerry, and Jim. There were so many of us, my mother planted a garden, so we picked and canned most of the summers. Fruit trees and berries kept our pantry full.

It was up in a green apple tree that my cousin Joyce said I told her about the birds and bees. Climbing trees and riding horses bareback became our usual entertainment. There were no cellphones or computers.

Our house was in the country on a dead-end road. In the winter, the snow would be waist deep. Sometimes when the bus could not get down our road, we would have to walk a mile to the main highway to catch a ride to school. Later when I told my children about walking in the snow because we loved school, they would say, "Oh, mom, not that story again about walking in waist-high snow for a mile."

When we were all old enough to work, we moved to town. It felt like we had moved to the city. This small Amish community was a flourishing village with Amish buggies coming into town for staples and hardware. They tied the buggies to a rail which surrounded the beautiful brick courthouse. The clicking of horses' shoes on the brick streets is a sound I have never forgotten.

My first job was at a Dairy Queen, which the Amish frequented. I learned to put the curl on and even manage the business when the owner went on vacation. My brother Don worked at a used car lot. Sister Dee worked at Magnavox. The two younger brothers, Jerry and Jim, were not old enough to work.

Our house in town was old with dark wooden floors and large rooms. The house still looks about the same as when we lived there. All of us left our small town for college when we finished high school. Now it is rare for us to get together, even for family reunions. We have scattered to distant states and have so many grandchildren to keep us busy. However, when we can see each other, we laugh and reminisce about olden days.

I was twenty-three, young and naïve, when I fell under the spell of a smooth-talking, seemingly well-off only child of a noted physician. The Bible says to be equally yoked, and I knew that, yet I ignored all of my earlier teaching. I was a cheerleader in high school and won a number of beauty contests. I thought I had the bull by the horns. I was brimming with self-confidence, but all that slowly changed. I had a feeling that all was not right before the wedding, but dismissed it as pre-wedding jitters. I acted my part at the wedding ceremony his parents and my mother wanted. The marriage was new, and things went well for several years.

My husband was a successful stockbroker. We had the home with the white picket fence we are supposed to dream about. After three children, he metamorphosed into an abusive alcoholic. I tried everything to make it work—thought it was my fault, tried to placate, and reduced myself to a subservient role. Nothing worked. I turned to the comfort of my religion, but when I talked to my pastor, he dismissed my plight with a flippant comment: "Don't worry, God will see him get better." Then my husband started hitting me. Once he hit me so hard under my left eye, it fractured the bone. Even now I have difficulty focusing in that eye. I caught him more than once with women in hotel rooms. I was being torn apart, but I had three young children and felt trapped.

Some people ask, "Why do you stay with a man who abuses you?" It is hard to explain, but I will try. The abuse does not happen all at once. It starts slowly. First there are a few words of abuse, then later he says, "I'm sorry." The next time it is the same thing all over again. Over the years, you start thinking you may have pushed the wrong button and must try to be better. You think, "If I make everything perfect—cooking, cleaning, and doing what he wants—it will be better." My self-esteem slowly disappeared.

I started attending a Bible study. Every week the friends I made encouraged me to get through another week. The more confident I became, the worse he got. The physical abuse started when his words didn't hurt me anymore. He started slowly with shoving and pushing. Then the bad stuff, black eyes and bruises, but then flowers came the next day! I excused his behavior by thinking he didn't mean it, he had just been drinking.

The kids and I would go to church Sunday morning, and when we returned home, he would have a bad attitude. Usually he had been drinking. This was always a bad sign.

One Sunday, I arrived home and started preparing lunch. Food sometimes helped his attitude. The kids were on edge, knowing trouble was brewing. He was in a bad state. I had baked a large cherry pie for lunch because it was Father's Day. The kids wanted a piece, but I said they would have to wait until after lunch. He walked into the kitchen and saw me working and heard the children talking about how good the pie would taste. He walked over, picked up the pie, and threw it in the garbage disposal. The kids were in tears. I was hurt, which is exactly what he wanted. The day was ruined. These are memories which never leave you. Behind closed doors, you never know what goes on. From the outside, neighbors and friends thought we were a perfect, beautiful family.

Finally, my children begged me to leave him. That was when I made up my mind to get a divorce. His father tried to intervene and offered me one million dollars if I would stay with his son. I refused. My husband was a stockbroker, and when he became aware of the pending divorce, he moved all our money to a safe hiding place.

Buckets of rain were falling. As I looked out my window, the questions Dr. Woods asked me continued to ring in my ears. When I realized I still couldn't see through the darkness obliterating memories of my first marriage, I knew I must have blocked out many of the painful things that happened to me. I don't think I will ever remember everything about my first marriage, even though we were married for twenty-one years and had three children together.

The divorce was quick and painless. I just wanted him gone. This was the first time we had peace in our house in years. Penniless and alone, I had three children to support. My ex-husband refused support, spending our money on what he wanted, and he stopped seeing the children. A psychologist friend said he probably had a borderline personality disorder. I was faced with earning a living for the four of us.

Having no money was extremely difficult, but I managed to work sixteen-hour days to make ends meet. I started a clothing design and retail store, and Anita Bryant became one of my best patrons. I admired her for the wonderful person she is. This country fell in love with her. She was America's sweetheart. For three consecutive years, *Good Housekeeping* named her "The Most Admired Woman in America." A Gallup poll listed her among the top ten women in the world. For twelve years, she was the spokeswoman for the Florida Citrus Growers, and for seven years, she was also the spokeswoman for Coca-Cola. She was the cohost for the Orange Bowl Parade eleven years, and appeared with Bob Hope seven years in his overseas Christmas shows for the US military.

There is much more, almost unbelievable. Anita is an entertainer-author-songwriter. She is also physically beautiful. She represented her native Oklahoma in the Miss America Pageant, becoming second runner-up. She appeared on nearly every major television show, including *Today, The Tonight Show, the 700 Club, 20/20, Larry King Live*, and *Hee Haw*. She has many honors, including Entertainer of the Year, first woman and youngest inductee into the Florida Citrus Hall of Fame and the Oklahoma Hall of Fame. She is also the winner of the Ellis Island Medal of Honor, the VFW Freedom Award, USO special awards, and three honorary doctor's degrees. She authored ten best-selling books and has three gold records, plus thirty albums. I could go on and on about this beautiful and caring person. We quickly developed a fast and long-lasting friendship.

Anita wrote about our friendship in her best-selling book, *A New Day*. She gave me permission to include what she said in her book.

> *"What about your wardrobe?" Bonnie asked me.*
> *"I don't know."*
> *"Anita, hosting a national television show like Pat Robertson's '700 Club' for a*

whole week means you have to update your clothes. Do you have what you need to do this job?"

"Well..."

Naturally Bonnie Brosius, an Atlanta fashion designer who operates two boutiques (Chabar) in upscale locales (I had met her when we moved to Atlanta) immediately would think about clothes. Her custom pieces look fabulous—simple, elegant, striking, straight forward as the designer. Now she stood before me, a determined look on her pretty face, and confronted my need.

"Let's make a deal. I'll travel with you that week and be your wardrobe mistress. We'll put your clothes together."

"But Bonnie, how can I pay you?"

"You can repay me some other way," she said firmly. "Anita, you need to learn how to barter."

Knowing Bonnie was like taking a course in Friendship 101, I thought. Our paths happened to cross soon after the kids and I moved to Atlanta, where we knew few people. I made the move for career reasons. By then I had been single for five years and had become used to coping with the many challenges single women face: driver's licenses for two kids, plus long-distance chauffeuring for their driver's education classes; my oldest girl Gloria, a college graduate now, back living with me and working; finding affordable housing and schools;

*running a household; earning a living—
you are familiar with the list.*

*With all that, who can afford the lux-
ury of friendships? Where would I find time?*

*Bonnie, I discovered, struggled with
those same problems and perhaps a few more.
Also divorced, she was a Christian, and a
woman with three children who had suffered severe rejection as well as physical and
emotional pain. Bonnie looked as fragile as
a Christmas-tree angel, but could work like
a horse. She has great inner strength and
a determination to follow Jesus. I saw she
meant business about living out her faith.*

*We made time for friendship. Here
was another "one-woman band," someone
who taught herself to design, purchase fab-
rics, cut, sew, merchandise, and run a business—and did much of that solo. Though
Bonnie was a newcomer to the fashion
scene, she recognized her talent and was
willing to bet on herself. She was exactly the
kind of model God knew I needed and I
know He directed our friendship.*

*Bonnie sustained me in certain ways,
I sustained her in others. We developed a
give-and-take relationship that became as
sturdy and dependable as a towering oak
tree. And gradually, Bonnie taught me one
of the most important lessons of my life:
although I had been going through this
painful course since my divorce, she taught
me to receive.*

Like many other performers, I never had enough time for many in-depth relationships. Travel, work, upgrading professional skills, enlarging my repertoire and maintaining the physical level needed to do such strenuous work—added to the pressing needs of husband, children, and home—left precious little time even to know myself, much less others.

All my adult life, I longed for day-to-day friendships like other women enjoyed. Instead of lunches or tennis dates with other women, however, I had to work with my music arranger, vocalize, or perhaps study terms of an upcoming concert booking. The schedule never quit. It owned me. Rarely could I steal time to do anything purely for pleasure. Even if I went shopping, or to a movie I felt guilty.

Once on my own, though, with those relentless career pressures behind me, at last I could form the friendships I had always yearned to enjoy. The problem was, I didn't always understand the ground rules.

For example, I've always enjoyed giving—everything from gag gifts, important gifts, parties, wonderful food, flowers and more flowers, you name it. Taking, however, was pretty much outside my experience. Now here was Bonnie, wanting me to accept items I could not afford to buy, extending herself when matters were as tough for her as they were for me.

Through Bonnie, I learned to receive. As she explained, friendship involves giving and receiving, and where you have just one side of that equation, you have a lopsided friendship. That seemed easy to say but hard to compute. I realize now that learning to receive from friends, humbling yourself, not having to occupy the driver's seat in the relationship, are essential lessons.

Even our Lord Jesus Christ humbled Himself to receive His human needs from the hands of ordinary people around Him. He had "no place to lay His head" (see Matt. 8:20; Luke 9:58), and His followers and friends—including many devout women—provided Him with food, hospitality, and lodging.

So here is Bonnie, a dynamite blonde who turns heads when she enters a room, but, more importantly, she is a radiant, practicing Christian. As time went on we bailed each other out a hundred times. We shared. We cried together, prayed together, complained together, and asked God a million times what was wrong with us. Why couldn't we get our acts together? Why weren't we successfully married? It turned out much later that the Lord answered our prayers for "His choice" of husbands. I had lunch with Cliff Flood, a tall, handsome airline pilot from Oklahoma; later I introduced him to Bonnie, and never dated him again. I teased them both unmercifully as I wished them well at their wedding reception. Her joy was mine!

Friends for 45 years

Cliff

As she mentioned above, after eight years of being single, Anita introduced me to this man from Oklahoma. After the experience with my first husband, I did not trust men. In business, I liked dealing with men, enjoyed talking to men, but to ever trust my emotions again seemed far removed. After four weeks and a number of phone calls from him, more to satisfy Anita than my own interest, I agreed to meet Cliff in August. He was just a little too smooth and too well-dressed. He was like a fashion model - six feet tall and built like the baseball player he had once been. It is said we all have a twin. Well he looked like Cary Grant with a mustache. Women drooled over him, wanted to talk to him, touch him. His eyes were the color of the winter sky when the snow clouds part, intelligent eyes that could look into the window of your soul. He was too overwhelming to be a real person, but gradually he tore down my wall brick by brick.

It was a beautiful sunny day, a perfect day for flying. Not a cloud in the sky. We were on our way to a private air strip to meet a large group of friends and pilots. This was a day of celebration for Cliff's retirement from the airline. He had been a commercial pilot for thirty-one years. When we arrived, we were greeted by many pilots, all admiring the beautiful planes landing. This was my first time meeting a lot of his friends. Some of them I had already met, and I liked them. The field was full of family and friends. It smelled like a county fair. The barbecue meat was cooking, and the tables were loaded with all the things that go with this kind of meal. After an hour, the line started to form for the food. All at once everyone started yelling and clapping. I had no idea what it was all about. They yelled to me to "Look up!"

When I looked up, I could not breathe. Someone said, "Are you okay?" I must have looked in shock. The plane flying over with a red-and-white banner read: "*Bonnie will you marry me? Love, Cliff.*" I could not speak for several minutes. Cliff took me by the hand and said, "That's okay, we will talk later."

Cliff's Proposal

On the way home with this gorgeous man and the magnificent sun setting, I said yes. I always said God would have to drop him from the sky. I think he did.

I called my pastor several weeks before the wedding and asked Jerry if he would marry me. He laughingly replied, "I would be glad to, but I am already married!"

After all my friends and family met Cliff, they gave me the thumbs up! When we finally made the commitment, it was full speed ahead. I only had a short time to prepare for the wedding. Friends and family would not settle for a "Quick, get married." I had waited a long time for my prince. This was going to be a wedding with all the bells and whistles. I quickly set my sewing room in a spin, making dresses for everyone in the wedding party, including mine. My sewing ladies were excited. We used pink silk with off-white lace

23

for the bridesmaids, my daughters, Deborah and Chari, and Cliff's daughter, Tracy. The clock was running down, but I had no doubt the sewing ladies would finish on time. My main sewing lady was very qualified. She had worked for a big designer in New York.

My dress was off-white lace with pearls and sequins and a large hat to match. We had green velvet for Anita, which was very becoming for such a beautiful lady. My mother was in pink lace. It was a fairytale wedding. The pink and red roses in large bouquets adorned the altar. The church was decorated for Christmas with red bows and garland. All was so perfect. Everything seemed to fall into place.

Anita sang *Phantom of the Opera*. I was so blessed to have my friend sing at my wedding. My son Michael looked so handsome in his tux, ready to give his mother away.

I was so nervous walking down the aisle, my knees were shaking, but as Michael gave Cliff my hand, I felt much calmer. Cliff had that way about him. He was always the calm in a storm. My best friends, Jerry and Brenda Howell, both pastors, jointly married us. Repeating the vows seemed to take hours. After the photos and signing the license, we were off to the reception.

Bonnie, Cliff, and Anita at Rehearsal Dinner

Bonnie and Cliff after Ceremony

Bonnie's White Lace and Pearl Wedding Dress

Bonnie, son Michael and Mom

Debra Dancing with Uncle Don

We closed Chao's restaurant in the Galleria mall. We installed a dance floor and had a jazz band. Our friends and family danced and rejoiced with us for hours. It could not have been a more perfect start for a fairytale life. We left for the airport and our honeymoon in Hawaii.

Bonnie and Cliff on Vacation in Hawaii

When we arrived back in Atlanta to our new home and family, it was another adventure. Every day was a joy in getting to know each other. Cooking together and entertaining our friends and family were some of our favorite things to do. Deborah soon learned to love Cliff. He was always ready to help her with any project. He would get her up for school with the smell of breakfast cooking. The Lord certainly knew what we needed by sending this man into our lives.

Deborah now had a kind, gentle father. There was peace in our home. One day Cliff asked, "Do you think Michael would like to live with us? We have plenty of room." When I asked Michael, he became very emotional and said he would love to live with us. This started a bond with Michael and Cliff that lasted thirty-one years. From that point on, Michael introduced Cliff as his father. Cliff was very proud of his new son and Michael's every success and accomplishment.

We married in December, and even after we married, I looked for chinks in his armor but did not find any. Finally I just let it all ride and started having the best time of my life. He displayed a sensitive, picking humor to my children. They loved his attention and adored him.

Before we married, we bought a pink house together in Marietta, Georgia. Coming home was a joy. Cliff talked me into closing my stores and travelling around the world. It was a wonderful time filled with peace and love. My daughter loved having a father in the house again. I tried so hard to be the perfect wife once again, and jumped up every minute to make sure he was pleased. I thought that was what a good wife does. One morning, he told me to stop, sit down, and let him get my coffee. I was shocked. It's hard to receive love when it had never been reciprocated before. For thirty years, he made my coffee. Every morning, he was awake before me. He would greet me, hug me, and hand me coffee. Oh, how I loved this beautiful man. We saw eight grandchildren born while we were married. They all called him Papa.

Bonnie and Cliff at Pink House

We were at a show for Anita when I received a call. My father had a heart attack. Cliff drove all the way back to Atlanta, picked up my kids and clothing, and drove back to Lexington, Kentucky, to be there for me. He was that kind of man. All my friends and family told me how much he loved me, and it showed.

But Cliff was more than just a "nice man." He knew our Lord. He revealed that to me on one of his commercial flights, his plane hit turbulent winds and began to descend in the darkness. He asked God for help. Just then he felt a hand on his shoulder. He thought the co-pilot had come back to the cockpit. He looked around and realized no one was there. He always felt it was divine intervention and the hand of God was on him.

I loved it when Cliff would call from the airport and say, "Get your bags packed. We're going to San Francisco tonight." He was a romantic, always putting me first. My favorite trip was when we went hiking in Switzerland. We prepared for three months in the rugged North Georgia mountains. I had no idea how to pack a bag for hiking. I was thinking I'd need all the girly stuff, like a curling iron, and I realized I was in trouble once we started on our trip. When you go hiking, you don't need a lot. We stopped in little villages for soup and homemade bread, yet we stayed in five-star hotels. Cliff knew I'd have trouble sleeping in the woods! We walked through fields of cows and sheep, and they ignored our intrusions. I have so many memories of places like this we have been which will last forever, but this was my favorite.

I was able to fly all over the world with him. We stayed in fine hotels, dined in fancy restaurants, and drove across whole countries. He truly was my prince in shining armor. For any problem, I would go find Cliff.

I began to get heavily involved in painting. With my palette and paints, when Cliff was flying, I roamed through the poppy fields of Van Gogh, with the morning sun scintillating through the poplars. For the first time in my life, I could let the magic of brush and paint come alive on canvas. I was happy.

I started to do oil paintings after I closed my stores. I opened a gallery and became hooked. As I continued to paint, I became interested in teaching art. I realized that I loved teaching more than painting, which led me to travel cross-country. One special student I had the privilege of teaching was President George W. Bush. One day I received a call saying I was requested to teach him for twenty-eight days in Boca Grande, Florida. Of course I said yes! He had so much passion for painting, it was a great joy teaching him. This was the highlight of my painting career, and it left me with many special memories. I have travelled to Boca Grande to teach now for nine years. My students have become dear friends.

Bonnie with President George W. Bush

Bonnie Painting

Cliff always brought me Flowers

Bonnie and Cliff on Cruise

CHAPTER 3

Paradise Lost

"In looking on the happy autumn fields,
And thinking of the days that are no more."
—Alfred, Lord Tennyson

The magic lasted for thirty-one years, which is more than most can claim in a lifetime. Cliff was diagnosed with pancreatic cancer. It was heartbreaking for all of us. After a great deal of research, we headed to Jacksonville, Florida, for treatment. Three months into treatment, his cancer had shrunk, and we had new hope he had been cured. One month later, he received the results of another MRI and found the cancer had actually spread to his liver. With prayer and much discussion, we decided to fight and do chemotherapy. After three sessions of chemo, loss of hair, swelling, and painful results, Cliff decided to stop the treatments. He said, "I want quality in the life I have left to live with the ones I love." We began the long, sad goodbye. He lived one year. He asked for communion two days before he died. He said he hated to leave me but couldn't wait to see the beautiful face of Jesus.

The day he died, the sun seemed especially bright. Light flooded his room. All our children and grandchildren laid on the bed with him, laughing, singing, and loving on him. He said he felt all of the love in the room, and he was in an enlightened spirit, cracking jokes and being very alert. At four-thirty in the afternoon, an ambulance came to take him to hospice. He winked at the family and waved. This was the last time our children saw him alive. At hospice, in his cheery voice, he told the nurses they were doing a great job. His last words will be forever embedded in my mind: At eight-thirty, he put my face in his hands and said, "You have always been so beautiful to me. I love you." At eleven-thirty, I heard the Lord take his breath away.

Weeks went by. I laid in a fetal position, crying for him and reaching to his side of the bed. Cliff was not there. There was nothing left. No warm body to snuggle close to—nothing.

Being a widow is a singular kind of displacement, completely different from any other kind of separation. No one can understand unless they are in the situation. When someone who has been divorced says to you, "I know how you feel," I just want to scream. "No, you do not! You chose a divorce. You had a loss, but your kids still have their father, and you still have an ex-husband. I am sure you might hate him, and you are sad, but at least he is still here, and you are able to move on." A widow is very protective when it comes to letting someone into their life, and you are vulnerable, like a rebound. I remember what it was like to be happy and joyful. I want to be that way again. Then I read the scripture in my devotion, where it talked about anxiety being great within me, but God's consolation bringing me joy. Cliff's favorite verse was, "This is the day the Lord has made. We will rejoice and be glad in it." This is the verse the pastor quoted on the evening of our wedding. We never forgot.

When Cliff passed away, Anita wanted to come to sing at the funeral, but I told her I would need her later. With all the family and friends, I would not have time to visit with her. Two weeks later, Anita flew to Atlanta from Oklahoma. We packed my car and headed to New Smyrna Beach. My friends Jim and Marty Boland let us borrow their condo for a week to rest and enjoy the beach. Our journey began with me driving and Anita serving as co-pilot.

I finally said, "Okay, Anita, you only tell me something if we are in danger. Just sit back and relax." We laughed all the way to the beach. Laughter is a good medicine. We had devotions every day, walked on the beach, and talked about past and future events.

One day I was taking Anita's picture when she was sitting on a rock. It had rained the night before so there were large puddles around the rock. When she stepped off into the water, she started to sink up to her waist. We laughed so hard, I could hardly pull her out. I do not know why everything seemed so funny. It was a great week for both of us. She was there at my wedding and comforting me now after Cliff's death. We have been best of friends for over forty years. We have grown old together, had a lot of laughter and a lot of tears. Our children have grown older and made us grandmothers.

Finding peace in the death of your spouse takes time. Some verses that may help you work out the plan for your life are Psalm 29:11, "The Lord gives strength to His people. The Lord blesses His people;" Psalm 46:10, "Be still and know that I am God;" and Isaiah 26:3, "You keep him in perfect peace, who's eyes have stayed on You."

Death reminds you life here on earth is short. Your faith will help you figure out how you feel about the afterlife and maybe leave a picture in your mind of where a loved one is. Some days I get a little angry. I talk to my husband, tell him my financial struggles and how hard it is. I tell him he is having a good ole time, and I am just down here. I ask him if he can hear me crying and if he feels how lonely I am. But then I remember Isaiah 43:16–19:

> *Thus says the Lord who makes a way in the sea, a path in the mighty waters, Who drew out the chariot and horses, the army and warriors, they laid down and never to rise again. They are extinguished, quenched like a wick. Forget not the former things nor consider the things of old. Behold, I am doing a new thing. Now it springs forth. Do you not perceive it? I will make a way in the wilderness and rivers in the desert.*

I discovered a new world, one I did not like and did not see coming. Being called a widow seems to take away part of your identity. It seems to define you to be "home alone." You become separated from your friends and even some of your family. It's as though you become half of a person. No longer whole, your friends forget about you. I think if I hear, "If you need anything, call me" again, I will lose it. I will personally never stand by and do nothing if one of my friends becomes a widow. Another thing they say is, "Sometime I will pick you up and take you to dinner." No one actually did that. So am I like a black widow now? It's easy for someone to pick up the phone and call, but to go out of your way and really be there takes thoughtfulness. Where is the church? Should they not help us through this? Others I've talked to have similar experiences, such as my friend, Jane:

As Jane prepared to pack and move, she started having second thoughts. Her husband had been gone for over a year. I am sure many widows can identify with what was happening to her and the dilemma. She wondered if his spirit was still there, in that house. She did not know if she was doing the right thing. There were boxes all over empty rooms. Throwing away stuff, maybe throwing away too much. Perhaps she would have regrets later, feeling like running away and taking nothing.

Jane's cat began doing strange things. She sensed something going on. She tore her litter box to shreds. She dug the litter out of the box until it was empty then clawed and bit the empty container. She made a strange, crying sound and raced out of the room to hide. Jane realized the reason for her actions. She too was feeling the tearing away of this life into a new, frightening one. Her actions matched Jane's feelings. Memories are all that's left. As she said, "I wondered if I would be happy moving many miles away. It could not be any worse than here. My friends have abandoned me. My family doesn't come or call. Scared, lonely, and frightened of a new start, I thought I would never be happy again.

"I roamed through the house, trying to remember the fun times we had here. I am hoping my new job will keep me busy and my mind free from despair and fill my empty days."

My sister Dee had a similar experience when she lost her husband, who also developed cancer. His health quickly deteriorated, and it was obvious that he was terminal. She tried to care for him at home, but eventually began to realize she needed help. She found herself alone as his caregiver, with no help from their children who didn't live close, or any of their friends. Her husband was also a retired airline captain and very independent, and she knew it was tough for him when he could no longer care for himself. Her life became difficult as well—none of their "couple friends" came around, so it was a lonely, sad time for her.

Finally, she knew it was necessary to put him in a facility for people who can no longer care for themselves. She went every day to be at his side and found herself exhausted. Cliff and I started to come by to help, and this gave Dee a little break. But there was still no sign of her old friends.

It was a touching time when her husband asked, "Why don't you go with me?" During this period, none of their old friends invited her to have dinner or lunch. If anything, they seemed to avoid her. Her husband passed away, and she became completely alone.

After reading my sister's story and thinking back on my loss, I began to see a common thread. It seems widows are "left behind" by their former friends. That was my motivation for writing this book. I wanted to find out if other widows and widowers experienced the same kind of rejection my sister and I felt.

I asked a male college professor to tell me his story of what it was like to lose a spouse of fifty years.

He wrote:

> *Linda sits quietly, not her usual uplifting personality. "I just hope they don't put that tube down my nose. I dread that the most of all." I try to be encouraging. "They are not going to do that because it's almost day surgery. Your doctor said I can take you home the following morning." This seems to make her feel better.*

Down the hall Linda presents her registration papers to the clerk in the glass enclosed office. "Upstairs, to the third floor," the clerk says, without looking at either of us. On the third floor a new feeling, one of almost old home day. Several nurses know either Linda or me or both. To some, Linda sold houses; some have been in my classes at the college years ago. Linda is smiling, always looking photogenic. On a moment's notice, Linda can spread a smile and look like she is ready for a photoshoot. Linda could be Elizabeth Taylor's sister. She has those same wondrous blue eyes, flawless skin, beautiful straight teeth and full black hair. She won several beauty contests in her teens, even going to the Biloxi, Mississippi, finals one year.

The doctor steps in for a brief visit and reassures us both it is a routine operation and we will be out of here the second morning. All sounds good. I can't wait to get her home and start taking care of her. We settle into her room. She looks at me with pleading eyes. "Don't leave me." It startles me because I have no intention of going anywhere.

"Don't worry, I wouldn't leave you for the world," I tell her. She seems to relax. The medication and IV fluids are helping dull her pain.

The hard vinyl chair reclines to an uncomfortable position, and nurses come and go with a flick of the light switch. The room has the iodoform smell of disinfectant and rubbing alcohol.

Finally, early morning light filters through the venetian blinds. An orderly and one nurse come into the room and announce, "Time to go, Mrs. Woods." The nurse barely glances in my direction when she says, "Come with us and I will show you where the waiting room is located. The doctor will see you there after the operation." My body begins to have intermittent cold sweats. Not really uncomfortable, not panic. I just want this to be over. I become upset anytime Linda is hurting. I always have to leave the room when a nurse puts an IV needle in her arm.

Several friends from our town are already in the waiting room. We settle in to talking and drinking coffee. One hour drifts by, which seems like ten. Finally the doctor, in his green scrubs, comes through the double doors. I quickly approach him, but do not say anything, waiting for him to speak. He does not seem concerned, which I take as a good sign. "The operation," the green knight says, "wasn't easy, but no complications. She will be fine." I don't hear anything else. I feel the tension drain from my body.

Everyone gathers around the good news. A scrub nurse comes out of the operating room and says my son and I can go back

43

to Linda's room. She will be there in about an hour. Again, I ask if she is all right. The nurse smiles and replies in the affirmative.

The orderlies wheel Linda's bed back into her room. Linda is still heavily sedated. It is crowded around her bed with different staff checking blood pressure, adding fluids to her IV. Much of the night she will wake and push her pain medicine button. I am instantly out of my chair to give her water or anything she wants.

The early morning sunlight sweeps the cobwebs from my brain after a sleepless night. Linda looks over to me, saying, "I am really in pain." This sends me into a cold sweat. Linda whispers, "I want to go home. I love home."

A nurse comes into the room to ask if Linda feels like walking down the hall. Linda props up on her pillows and says she will try. She slides off the side of the bed and holds on to the nurse's arm. The two of them slowly walk to the corner of the hall and past. She is out of sight for a few minutes and seems stronger when she rounds the corner. I sigh; she is getting better. I thank God silently.

During the night I remain at her bedside because the pain never seems to stop. Once she looks at me and asks me to kiss her. I lean over and gently press my lips to her cheek.

Midmorning, two nurses enter the room looking anxious. They begin unhook-

ing monitors and start to roll her out of the room. One nurse says the doctor sent orders for Linda to go to ICU. I watch as they push the bed down the hallway. Linda looks back over her pillow, trying to see me. I walk back to the waiting room. My son gets there about the same time I walk in.

Two hours later the surgeon comes back through the swinging doors. He glances up with a "come hither" look at my son and me. He says he needs to operate again because Linda is not responding like he expected. With no thought, I blurt out, "She is not going to die, is she?"

Without making face contact, the doctor mumbles, "I hope not." My heart palpitates wildly and I feel faint, as a sense of terror and doom grabs me. I am having trouble breathing, and I feel chest pains. I can barely whisper, "Please don't let her die; she is all I have." The plea is half to the doctor and the other half to God. I am powerless. I have no control. Nothing is in my hands.

Our friends fill the room. They assure me she is going to be all right. I only half hear. My mind is in overdrive. "What if she dies?" No, no, I must get her home and take care of her, pet her, do everything for her. We always said we would go together. Neither believed we could live without the other. What would be the point? Thoughts raced back to Linda jokingly saying, some women want their husbands to be happy but not her. She could not stand the thought of another woman taking her place. Linda said recently, several times, the one thing she regretted about our marriage is that, we did not get married sooner. She joked, I think, saying if she ever knew she was going to die, I had better hide the guns. It will be all right with me. I don't want to face life without her. She was my motivation even before I met her. The one thing I wanted in life was a woman—not just any woman but one with movie-star looks, a smart, sweet personality, and someone who wanted to be a partner. Linda is all of these and more. She is God's gift to me. I don't know why he gave me such a life-fulfilling gift, but he did. Surely he is not going to let her be taken from me. I have nothing to offer without her.

The surgeon appears again in the double doors. He does not have time to motion for my son or me. We are by his side in an instant. He uses some medical technical terms and says we can go into ICU to see her.

We walk into her station, and my brain instantly screams, "No!" The tubes she dreaded so much are inserted in her nose and down her throat. She mumbles incoherently. Her eyelids are closed over her beautiful blue eyes. I rush out of the room, turn, and go back in. She's had operations before, but this time I know she is in deep trouble. The orderly says we have to leave.

Our pastor, friends, and daughter-in-law are in the waiting room. This is my third day at the hospital. My son and others say I need to go to the house, take a shower, change clothes, and come back. It is going to be a long vigil. It will be two hours before my son and I will be allowed back in ICU.

I take their advice and drive as fast as possible, in and out of the shower, dress, and almost make it to the parking lot when my cellphone rings. All I can think to say is, "Is she dead?"

"No," my son says. "Where are you?"

I reply I will be there in five minutes.

The orderly comes to the waiting room. He says the only thing keeping her alive is the breathing machine. "Do you want us to take her off of it?"

"No! God, no!" The thoughts stomp through my brain. I look at my son. "Dad, she is already gone," he says sadly. "The machine is doing her breathing for her."

I look at the orderly and ask, "If she were your wife, what would you do?"

He is all business. "I would stop the artificial method of putting useless air into her body." Linda dies.

My world is over, why am I still breathing? Part of me is dead, surely the other half will follow. The hospital will not let me see her. Lethargic, in a state of shock, I am driven home by a friend. We see people on the sidewalk, meet traffic. Why does

*the world not stop? Don't they understand
Linda is dead!*

*The family doctor, a long-time friend,
sends several pills to the house. I cannot
resist anyone. I have no will of my own.
What anyone says, I do. My son takes me
to the funeral home to pick out a casket,
make arrangements—everything one must
do. My daughter-in-law picks out the casket
and chooses the flowers. Even the funeral
home will not let me see Linda. She is not
"ready," they say. My son contacts one of
his friends to purchase a grave plot. Linda
and I had made no arrangements for death.
One thing for sure, I refuse to let her be put
in the cold, wet earth far from me. My son
again has a friend who can order an above-
ground tomb from Italy.*

*I didn't know if I could make it
through visitation, but the people who
know Linda start lining up, and I can't
wait to hug them and listen to them say
good things about Linda and to remember
a happier time. For hours, the townspeople,
colleagues, and friends from church file into
the sanctuary. On the wall, a projector dis-
plays picture after picture of Linda through-
out her life. She is so beautiful, and I am so
proud of her. Visitation is over too soon.*

*I cannot sleep. I swallow several of the
little blue pills my doctor friend sent me.
I am in the funeral home early. There are
papers to sign, bills to pay, and two lots in*

the cemetery to purchase. Before the funeral, the director asks the family to have a private meeting with Linda. There are only five of us, my son, daughter-in-law, two grandchildren, and me. I ask for the casket to be opened for one last moment with Linda before she is gone for all eternity. I lean over the side of the casket and kiss her on her cheek. I back slowly away, and they close the lid forevermore.

Linda is placed in a mausoleum until her tomb in the cemetery arrives. A special reinforced concrete slab is poured to support the coming weight. The granite tomb weighs six-and-one-half tons. I go every day, sometimes two or more times to visit, to touch the hard stone, knowing my hands are only inches from her body. I talk to her. I know it is a one-way conversation, but it helps me. The faith I have keeps me somewhat sane.

The next few weeks I walk around in a stupor. I find myself searching "out" others who have lost a mate, both male and female, but mostly males, since I can identify with their state of mind. There are plenty of activities to keep me busy—a pool shooting group on Monday nights, church on Sunday, a dinner group on Friday nights, and routine chores like opening the mail, visits to the bank, trips to the grocery store, laundry, eating out. I now do things Linda always took care of, and everywhere I go, I go alone. We were always thought of as Linda and Wayne, now it is just Wayne. Several times a day, I dial Linda's office number to hear her voice on the answering machine. I imagine a familiar image of her sitting at her desk, all professional, looking beautiful. Linda never seemed to age. I smile before I cry. One bedroom upstairs becomes a shrine to Linda. Her pictures adorn the room, starting when she was one year old: high school pictures, photos of her in evening dresses in beauty pageants, pictures of us together, pictures of my son with us, then pictures of my son and daughter-in-law's wedding, and finally pictures of the two grandchildren.

    Linda, it seems, waited all her life for these two grandchildren. She sat for hours on the den floor having a tea party with the little granddaughter while our grandson and I chased each other through the house for an ambush with Nerf guns. It's all gone— the laughter and smell of cookie dough. The rooms are empty tombs, devoid of life.

    Once, coming home from lunch at the country club, I started to cry. I read somewhere you should not hold back and just let yourself cry it all out. I just let go. I drove into my garage with tears streaming down my cheeks. I could not stop. I lay down on the couch but could not breathe. I try desperately to keep from hyperventilating. I seem to have no hope, just waiting on the kindness of death. I think I am having a heart attack. Instead of calling for an ambulance, I call my son. He is an EMT.

He arrives in about five minutes. He has a calming presence. I slowly regain control and calm down. I know I cannot let myself go like this again.

A few weeks later I am sitting in my office feeling sorry for myself when a thought, just a quick glancing blow of a memory trace, races through my brain. Like an old west movie theme, I could run away. I am sure thousands of people all over the country wish they could just run away from it all at some point in their lives; however, my thoughts have some reality. I thought of a time, a long-ago time, more than fifty-two years in the past, when I found myself high up in the rocky mountains of New Mexico. Perhaps there is still magic, a new spiritual awakening for me. Like Scarlett O'Hara, it is the land calling me back to a time before love and pain. I worshiped the ground Linda walked on, but here might be a door, a small porthole created out of total despair. I find myself packing to spend three months living in a tent, to work at a large New Mexico ranch and camp. I will look for others who will come like myself to escape the dark side of life. We all are looking to replenish something lost. I am looking for the old magic, a time of spiritual connection with mountains reaching to the sky, searching for God.

51

In Elisabeth Kubler-Ross's book *On Death and Dying*, she theorized five stages every grieving person must go through—denial, anger, bargaining, depression, and finally acceptance.

However, despite the popularity of this five-stage theory, they don't hold up. Most people accept the loss right off. Trying to go through the stages might actually cause more trauma. What really works is to get up and start moving. Knowing how other people have put their lives back together and become happy again can help. You have to find what works for you. Don't try to copy someone else's method. Start by doing something you love, something you enjoy. It does not matter how you think you should act or feel and, worse, not how you think others might judge you. Do what feels good and hang the guilt.

CHAPTER 4

Seeking a New Life

Nothing can bring you peace, but yourself.
—Ralph Waldo Emerson

In James 1:27, it clearly says, "Pure and undefiled religion before God and the Father is this: to visit the fatherless and widows in their affliction, and to keep one's self unstained by the world." In North America, our society fails to do this. Many widows have been left out of society. Over eight hundred thousand people are widowed each year in this country. There are fourteen million widows in the United States, which averages out to be at least fourteen widows in each church. It is important for churches to be aware of their needs. So many people die within six months of being a widow because they are friendless and lonely. Losing their friends and their support are the main factors, along with neglect of themselves. Poverty among widows is higher among most elderly women.

Some Indian tribes, when a woman's spouse dies, leaving her without a hunter and a partner to take care of each other, she becomes a burden to the rest of the group. Members of her tribe take her belongings and give her a small bowl of food and container of water. The tribe moves on to leave her to die, helpless and alone. Our culture is much too sophisticated for this. We have a place "for mom."

Widow groups are often led by someone who is not a widow and cannot fathom the circumstances, having no personal experience to be leading these groups. The leader should survey the group and find their biggest needs. Financial needs and upkeep on living space are common problems. Having connections to friends is like medicine. This journey is a time where a widow needs caring and believing people near her. A list should be made for each widow for all numbers and names of real people who can and are willing to help.

When I moved from my home, my children helped me, but no volunteering from my friends. After losing a spouse, most widows become more passionate and stronger in their faith. I am ashamed to say I never thought of a widow with such compassion until I became one. Could I have helped someone?

One week before Cliff passed, he informed me that we were completely broke. I had no idea because he always took care of everything, and I just did what I loved to do, which was being an artist. We were broke due to bad investments unknown to me. He had dropped his life insurance because he could not afford to pay for it. This was devastating, and after the funeral, reality hit hard. I had to sell our home. If it was not for my faith and strong attitude, I don't know where I'd be. Painting and my personal connections kept me afloat. Going through all of our papers and files, trying to find passwords and billing information, I sat on the floor in the upstairs office, seeking out some kind of truth.

I speak to all women now: Speak to your spouse about precautions to take when they are gone. Know your passwords, finances, and legal documentations.

I set out to find a gallery space where I could teach art. I located a place in Alpharetta, Georgia, about forty minutes from home. With hard work and a personal, punched time clock, I had the space fixed up and ready to go. Cliff's words echoed through my mind as I did this. Before he died, he told me to sell the house, move to Avalon, and figure out what I wanted to do with the rest of my life. That sounded good to me. The house was too much upkeep for me, and I needed to be around people. The Atlanta area was just what I needed.

Cleaning out the house was hard. I cried over his clothes and pictures. I cried again as I put his shirts and his beautiful blue housecoat in a bag for Goodwill, to be worn by someone else. Everything I gave away tore his memory from me. His cologne and other personal little things reminded me of how much I missed his sweet touches and soft embraces. Now the closet was only mine. I needed to get out of the house and feel nothing. The house made it impossible not to visualize him walking around and sitting in his favorite chair. I found a note in some of his papers he had written about me, but not to me. It still makes my cry when I read it:

> *When I look at a beautiful flower, I think of another beautiful thing that God created, the most important part of my life, you! More important than the physical beauty is the inner person. You are a beautiful person, Bonnie, considerate of other people's feelings, wanting to share their bur-*

dens, and so willing to offer comfort and help to anyone with a need.

Every day I think of what God did for me, and I give Him thanks. I was alone and lonely and I asked him for someone to love and someone who would love me, and God put us together in the strange and wondrous ways His miracles are performed. He surely loves me a lot to have answered my prayers.

Every day I ask the Lord to forgive me when I have fallen short in the way a husband should treat his wife. I love you more than I can describe. I know that sometimes I am difficult and short of patience, and I am always aware of this afterwards and am sorry. I promise to try more. I would never intentionally hurt you in any way. I know I do and am always sorry. Please remember how important you are to me. I love you, Bonnie.

Cliff

The day I moved into my small apartment, my daughter Deborah and her two daughters, Rachel and Sarah, unpacked everything as I sat numbly on the couch. The small space made me feel I was on vacation in a hotel. However, I was only five minutes away from my gallery. I walked to dinner by myself. It was getting less lonely, until I saw people walking and holding hands.

It had been over two years since Cliff died, and I thought I was ready for companionship and the next chapter of my life. I joined an online dating site. I received pointers on what to say about myself from my twenty-two-year-old granddaughter, Sarah. I got a smiley face emoji from someone for the first time, which was neat. He said he was five-ten. He lied. We were nose to nose. No chemistry on that one.

The second guy arrived with a mason jar full of flowers from his garden. We didn't have any common interests. He was a nice guy, just not my type.

The third gentleman I met for coffee, so I could have a quick getaway. I was learning how to do this thing. He was divorced and talked about his terrible ex-wife. I didn't want to help him carry around that baggage. I deleted him from my contacts, but the coffee was good.

The fourth guy I gave a shot to was very handsome. His wife died from the same kind of cancer Cliff did. I thought for sure we'd have a lot in common. I told him the details about my life, and then it was his turn.

As he talked about his beautiful wife and how much pain she went through, he started crying. The more he talked about her, the more he cried. He cried for twenty minutes. So I put my arm around him and told him I didn't think he was ready for me. He agreed.

I met another good-looking, tall man on this site, and that one was actually tall in person. He seemed interesting, and we exchanged phone numbers. That was months ago. We still talk every night. Not only is he interesting, but a very kind, good Christian man. We visited each other, and he is a widower of over three years. He is from Alabama, so I call him Alabama.

When I feel really lonely, I call Anita. She's the one who introduced me to Cliff. She gives me a shot of "You can do it.

You are a child of the King." I find it makes perfect sense to lean on these fruitful people when in need, and to trust God will place the right person in my life when it is time.

I continued to talk to other widows about their experiences. I thought I was all alone with this sad feeling, and maybe there was something wrong with me, but I came to find out other widows had been through the same kind of thing. The first widow I spoke with, we will call Joan.

Joan has been a widow for four years. She is a beautiful woman who was married for fifty years to a man she fell in love with at seventeen. She is an artist and interior designer. She had two sons with her husband, and they had many friends. After his death, she also felt alone and rejected. She decided to help herself and do something about it.

She started dating a few men, but was only left disappointed because of the comparison between these men and the fifty years of strong love she had experienced with her husband. I am a little worried about Joan. She is extremely attractive, and younger men see her beauty. She works out every day and takes good care of herself. She is very comfortable financially. I was curious to see if she could truly be happy again.

One day, she finally knew she was ready to date again. She was walking through Neiman Marcus and saw a naked male mannequin. She got excited and realized what she was missing in her life.

Joan also told me another great story. She ran across her husband's number in her phone. She went ahead and called it to see what would happen. A man answered and said, "Hello? Who is this?"

She quickly replied, "Joe? You've forgotten me!" He said he wasn't Joe.

Talking with Andie brought tears to my eyes. She told me about her life and what she had been through as a widow. She is an attractive forty-five-year-old dancing instructor. Her relationship with her husband was a rollercoaster ride. He was riding a motorcycle in the mountains when a pickup truck drove him off the road. The truck did not stop. Hours passed before someone saw him and called for help. He had back surgery with many days of pain, but with the help of rehab, he seemed to recover. Then a bigger problem occurred. Her husband became hooked on pain killers. Each new doctor prescribed another pill. Andie tried to keep her job and take care of their children. Her son Tommy sometimes did not come home at night. One night she received a call from the police department, asking her to come to the police station. They found Tommy in a back alley. He had overdosed and was dead.

Andie is trying to recover, and has decided to move near her family for support. Her friends quit coming by. They are just too busy. She is dealing with this harshly and feels so much blame. She has had some suicidal thoughts.

Suicide is a significant global concern. Some eight hundred thousand people take their own lives every year. For every person who commits suicide, there are at least sixty individuals intimately and directly affected. Andie has health issues, but maybe the move will bring some kind of closure for her and her children.

It seems there are a lot of widows in Florida. One in particular fascinates me. She has four homes from Jackson Hole, Wyoming, to Boca Grande, Florida. She was married seventy years and met her husband in the eighth grade. He graduated from Brown and became a lawyer. She worked with a travel agency to put him through law school. When her husband graduated, he worked for a small law firm. He believed he would be drafted, so he joined the Navy. He soon became a commissioned lieutenant. It was a great experience for both of them. She became pregnant with their first child, and four years later, they moved back to Michigan, where he eventually started his own law firm. This was remarkable for a man who started out with nothing. They soon had four children and prospered in life with numerous friendships.

Her experience was totally different from mine once her husband passed. She mourned for a few months and then decided she would no longer allow herself to be alone, so she surrounded herself with couples and friends. She went out of her way to initiate connections, and it worked, and it was reciprocated. She believed it was our responsibility to contribute to relationships. She still owns the family business and makes decisions. Her life is filled with friends and community involvement, although she has not dated. She said she wouldn't mind having a companion for dinner and conversation.

Jane married her high school sweetheart, although they had both been married before. Their first marriages ended in divorce. Her second husband developed cancer and died. She gained the title of mother to her late husband's children and grandchildren. Her friends abandoned her as though she had the plague. She is a beautiful lady. She wondered why all her friends abandoned her. She was lucky to get invited to a party where she met a man. She hesitated to let him into her life, but now they are happily married. She still carries resentment for the rejection of her friends. Joyce had a similar experience:

> *I am a widow. My husband of more than forty years passed away almost twenty years ago. We lived in a really small town where I taught school and my husband owned a real estate company. We had many close friends. Our very best friends were composed of six couples. We did everything together—dinner, movies, dancing, cruises, and more. My wonderful husband lived only twelve weeks after he was diagnosed with stage-four cancer. All of our friends were supportive during those twelve weeks. I could always count on them for their support. But I soon found grief and friendship don't go together. Friendships are immune to grief. When I needed my friends the most, they weren't there. At first, my friends supported me, but as the weeks passed, the support came to an end. They did not invite me out on the weekends anymore. Occasionally, I would have lunch with some of them, but that soon ended. I was on my own!*

When I was in town, silence fell when my friends saw me, as they were unsure how to treat me. I began to realize my friends didn't want to listen to my pain or grief. So, as a result, I started to try to be more upbeat. But sadly, this was moving on too quickly. As a result, I decided to move to another state where people only knew me as one and not as a couple. This worked for a little while with my new friends before they started pulling away. This made me realize I needed to have single friends. Was I a threat to married couples? Did couples find being around me uncomfortable? Was I a threat to their marriages? None of the above was true, but it did not encourage friendships with couples. I'm not sure if my friends knew what to say to me or how to help me. I didn't need this at all. I just needed my friends! Being a widow has helped me realize that I need to be a more caring person to others going through a loss. I have adjusted, but still miss people, and don't understand why I was left alone to face my grief.

Widowhood is not contagious, and you can't catch it. Please don't believe I'm grieving so much I might not be fun at your dinner party. If I move on too quickly, do not judge me. Don't tell me I haven't waited long enough. Life goes on, and there are better days, which softens the bad ones. There are no rules to follow, and losing your spouse is different for every individual. You can't feel guilty for the rate of time it takes to recover. Some widowers or widows bring upon themselves a self-imposed isolation, feeling as though they do not belong with other couples. The average age of a widow is fifty-five. People who have lost a spouse have usually been through a lot of caregiving and have wound up letting themselves go while caring for their loved one.

The widowhood effect is a very strange thing. One research study I read recently showed fifty widows out of five hundred died within three months of their spouse, twenty-six died within three to six months, and forty-six died within six to twelve months. The aftermath is the strongest within the first three months, with a sixty-six percent chance of the widow dying within a few years. The cause is grief and lack of personal care during the illness of the spouse. Support from family and friends is the key to a widow or widower living longer and starting a new life. The world was made for couples, and it is very difficult to be alone in the world.

Nancy, a widow of three years, said she is even left out of family gatherings. It was bad enough when friends left, but when her family stopped including her, it really hurt. She has a sister who she and her husband visited often. Since her husband's death, she does not get invited to events involving other family members. She sees things on Facebook of others visiting her sister, hears of social gatherings, but she does not get an invitation. She does not know if it's her sister's choice or her sister's husband. She and her sister have so much in common, but she cannot seem to find an answer to this problem.

As I search for answers to widowhood, I am amazed at churches that do not offer a program for us. When I asked that question to the woman who answered the phone at one church, she responded by saying, "Well, no, we minister to all people." She asked me not to quote anything she said. This is why I am attempting to find some answers for this hurting group of people. There are eight hundred thousand new widows each year. We need churches to give back. One individual said Christianity is the only religion which kills their wounded. While I do not believe this, I do think churches can do more.

Ruth 1:16–17: I just read about Ruth again in the Bible. It is a story about love and commitment. Ruth would not be

torn away from her widowed mother-in-law, although Ruth was also a widow. She said to her mother-in-law:

> *Where you go, I will go. Where you lodge, I will lodge. Your people shall be my people and your God my God. Where you die, I will die and there I will be buried. May the Lord do so unto me and more if anything but death parts me from you.*

God blessed Ruth with a wealthy man who took Ruth as his wife and also took care of her mother-in-law. If all people did that for each other, there would not be as much need for nursing homes for mom. I puzzled over why they advertise a place for mom but no place for dad? This is the answer I find most often: "Mom can't stay with me. She is more needy than Dad. She will get into stuff and offer advice, but Dad will be quiet, and it doesn't bother him to be left alone."

Korean widows are taken in by their children, which leaves them to enhance their social networking and protects them from depression. During the marriage, the wife is responsible for her husband. After the death of her husband, she is once again ready for responsibility. The widower has less of an issue when he loses his wife because, just like in America, he tends to remarry quickly to find another caregiver. The widow moves in with her children, which eliminates some of the effects of grieving; therefore, longer life is more common.

In the Japanese culture, a number of Japanese widows are choosing to terminate legal relations with their in-laws after the death of their spouse. The history is for the widow in Japan to be taken care of by her in-laws, but more and more women are breaking ties with their mother-in-law to free themselves from any responsibility for her.

I am constantly learning new things interviewing widows and widowers. I had an appointment with two widowed sisters. Their husbands died within months of each other. They are both are in their early eighties. Upon arriving, I was met at the door by a lovely lady and a barking dog. Emily was happy to see me and eager to tell her story. Two cats are curled up on the sofa. The dog, finding me friendly, calms down. The home is very neat and well decorated. Many family photos are all over. Emily's sister is full of smiles and greets me with, "Would you like tea?" There is a tray of cookies with the tea. Jane tells me how grateful she is to have her sister. They are both on Social Security. This is their only source of income.

Emily says the only solution for them was to move in together. Living in a small town for years makes it easy for them to arrange this new home together. They live a very comfortable life. Their church provides transportation to services. They walk to the grocery store and travel to special events with the church. They have each other to lean on, and they have many church friends.

I have learned many people choose to live together, rather than risk losing their deceased husband's Social Security. If you have been married for ten years, you may collect Social Security on your deceased husband, but if you remarry you may not. The same goes for a divorced person. You can always choose your own Social Security. So I found a good number of people chose to just live together. After you reach sixty, you may collect Social Security from your deceased spouse even if you do remarry, but those under sixty will not receive their spouse's Social Security if they decide to remarry.

One lady told me she is thirty years old and from New York. Her husband died of lung cancer several years ago. She said the symptoms occurred one evening when they were having a date night out dancing. Suddenly he grabbed his head in pain and felt dizzy. The next day, after an MRI, their lives changed. The lung cancer had moved to the brain, and they were expecting their first child at Christmas. It was September, and they wondered if her husband would be there for the birth of their son. They talked about her future, and made a video for the son to be seen when he got older. She started crying, saying her husband would not see her beautiful son grow into a man. She and her son watch the video of "Daddy" often. It is her son's favorite thing to watch. She said she will make it. She thanks God for a son who looks exactly like his father. She said she could count on family, but their friends seem too busy, but that's alright. Her son takes up most of her time. She thinks one day she will date again, but not now. Her son and church are her priorities.

Mary Ann called me when she heard I was writing a book about widows and life after the devastating loss. She said she had a love story and did I want to hear it. I beamed, because of course I could never turn down a good love story. Mary Ann was a flight attendant and had been married for fifteen years. She was on a long international flight with a long layover. She loved her job, which gave her a lot of time with her six-year-old son and her husband, with a few days of flying every month. Her husband Jack worked for a local bank. Jack loved all the benefits his wife received from her job. Her mother always helped out with the babysitting when she was flying.

Jack and his friends went deep-sea fishing one weekend she worked. He knew after having fun and drinking, he should not drive, but he was running late and needed to get back home so her mother could leave.

On the way home, he crossed the middle line and hit a big truck. He was killed instantly. When Mary Ann arrived at the airport terminal and saw her family, she knew they had bad news. Mary Ann collapsed when she heard. Her world came to an end that day. It would be six months before she could do normal things again. It was only her son who gave her a reason to live. It would be a year before she could go back to work. Even then her first flight was a nightmare.

She worried about her son, but she knew her mother would take good care of him. Several flights later, she started talking with a pilot, and found he had been divorced for three years.

On her next flight, she saw him again. He asked her to dinner on their layover. Mary Ann needed the company and someone she could talk to. He told her she had been constantly on his mind since the first time they had talked. She felt the same, but did not want to think it was more than friendship.

Several dinners later and visits with each other, it was apparent it was more than a friendship. The pilot and Mary Ann blended their families. Her son was seven by this time, and the pilot had a ten-year-old daughter. Moving was not a problem for her. They both continued to fly and have been married for four years.

CHAPTER 5

The Casserole Parade

Kissing don't last; cookery do!
—George Meredith

Men seem to have a different experience. They are the "poor widower who doesn't eat right," so they get invited to everything. After a sixty-year marriage, Rachel's father became a widower. The very day his wife died, ladies started bringing casseroles. Women called to see what they could do to help him. There were so many casseroles, he had to give them away. He must have been quite a catch. One lady even borrowed a ladder and climbed on his back deck to show him how interesting she was.

Henry lives in a retirement community for those fifty and older. He tells me there are so many widows, he can take a different one out every day of the month. This fits the eight-to-one ratio just about right.

I am very interested, so I ask him, "Do they all know that you do this?"

He says, "Yes, but they try to outdo each other, making cookies, cakes, and dinner." Henry says he doesn't cook anymore. His wife died a year ago. The entourage of women started immediately upon his moving into this community. Welcome casseroles started his first day. He admitted his grieving time was cut short with all the attention.

I ask if there was a special one he liked more than any of the rest. He replied in the affirmative, but said she is not as attentive as the others. I ask a question you are not supposed to ask a newly widowed person: "Do you ever want to get married again?"

His answer: "Why should I? I have a harem here!"

I ask him if he had been like this in his youth. He said he actually was very shy and was faithful to his wife of forty-five years. I suggested if he stopped his roaming from one to another, he might get the attention of the one he really liked. He responded, "Not anytime soon! I am having too much fun."

My next interview was with a man who was having the opposite experience of Henry. I met Jack by the fountain in the park. He told me on the phone he would be wearing a western hat, blue shirt, and cowboy boots. He sounded like what I would call a dude. When I arrived at the fountain, I couldn't miss him.

There was mister "home on the range," all decked out. I was not sure if this was his normal attire, or maybe he took the information that I was leaving shortly for my favorite place on earth, Santa Fe, New Mexico, and wanted to impress me. He did not seem comfortable talking to me, but he gave me his story anyway.

He moved to Atlanta from Michigan two years ago. He said he came for the Georgia women, but had not met a native Georgia woman yet. He indicated the bar scene was his way of "hooking up."

I asked if he had tried any singles sites or groups in Atlanta. He replied he tried several with no luck. One group would not let him come back to their meetings. He would not say what he did to be barred. I think it might have been his cowboy outfit.

We talked for thirty minutes more about church, family, and his ex-wife. He said his mother suggested counseling. She said she would pay for the sessions if he would go. He was thinking about it. He was also planning to go back home to Michigan.

Jim and Amy were married for twenty-five years and had three children. Then Amy was diagnosed with breast cancer. The cancer spread fast, and she died. Jim faced the burden of having no wife and three girls. He started dating once again after a year and a half. It was too much pressure to date women with young children. He finally found a widow who was a good match. His friends started backing off, because they felt he was being disloyal to his wife, but fifty was too young to be single. The casseroles had stopped coming. After a few months, he told the girls about the woman. He was surprised to have them say they thought it was great. The oldest of the sisters gave her other siblings the thumbs up, and they all believed that no one needed to cry all the time.

It was okay to love again.

A person may be sad, but they don't need to be miserable. The main idea a person needs to learn is, "What do you want to do?" Keep in mind you are responsible for you. Once you accept this, it takes away much of the power you have allowed others to have over what you think of yourself and what you want to do.

Widowed eight years ago, Jake had been his wife's caregiver for over six years. He did have a lot of support, but old friends started disappearing. The casseroles did too. His friends became those in the grief groups. He said he became a fifth wheel, and even if invited to something, you were left confused and lonely. He used the analogy of grief as a big storm. The ocean and giant waves become close together over time. The height of the waves soon subside. The waves always return, but with less intensity. Occasionally there is a large one, caused by anniversaries, birthdays, and other important dates. He said you adjust to being alone but never to the loneliness. He dates a little but has not found anyone who fits the profile he is looking for.

Depressed individuals may search years for that magic rope that will lift them from the enveloping quicksand to the golden staircase of self-fulfillment. Is this ever going to happen? Possibly, but unless the individual is open to changing his or her behavior, it probably will not. It is a shock when a spouse dies. Then the grieving person begins to realize their spouse is gone forever, and there is nothing left of them. Rebuilding can start only after this realization. It is okay to be sad, but the bereaved should not be miserable. They should be able to think of the dead person without being overwhelmed with remorse.

Jan's story: "My husband, two boys, and myself relocated to Charleston, South Carolina, for career growth opportunities and the social and cultural events the city offers. Friends and family visited often to enjoy the ocean, boating, and good life the low country has to offer. Our home was a destination location long before the world knew about 'the great state of Charleston...a state of mind.'"

Then Jim died of cancer. His death brought an outpouring of concern by family, friends, church, and others. Her immediate family and best friends have and continue to be there for her. Over the first six months, a handful of friends invited Jan to brunch. She attended fellowship gatherings sponsored by the church. As time lapsed, a smaller handful of friends remained close, and they connected regularly. As for others, there was small talk. She said, "I am blessed. I awake to see the sunrise. I walk on the beach. I devote time with the Lord to be comforted, amazed, humbled, and grateful. I feel God has plans for me in this next phase of my life's journey. I am steadfast, as eternity is only a breath away."

John went on a cruise to get over a recent breakup. He had met a woman four months after the death of his wife of thirty-five years. It was too fast and too soon for him. He was devastated when she told him she did not want to see him anymore, because she had met someone she liked better.

John had gotten emotionally involved too quickly after his wife's death. He was trying to fill the hole she left with someone else. It didn't work for him. He decided to take a cruise to help clear his mind.

During the cruise, John realized he needed to mourn his loss. He began to slowly breathe in the fresh air and walk

paths on the islands of Hawaii. He finally started acknowl-
edging his loss. Denial was John's problem. He had no children. His grief was his alone. He discovered he had tried to
escape his pain with a new lady, but now he knew it wasn't
real. It had only been a cover up for his real feelings. In releas-
ing his feelings for his wife, he started to heal. We all want to
escape, but there comes a day when we have to face the loss.
It is better to do it now, not later.

Studies have shown healing from grief is quicker and
more complete when the marriage was happy, but those with
unhappy marriages have higher bouts of depression, anxiety,
poor health, and yearning for years after the spouse's death.
If the spouse mourns for an extended period of time, they
will probably show a variety of physical complaints such as
insomnia, headaches, back pain, loss of appetite, indigestion,
shortness of breath, and maybe heart problems.

Lillie invited me for coffee one morning to tell her story.
The front door of her home was very inviting, painted a rosy
red with a beautiful spring wreath hanging on it. Flowers
planted around in pots brought a smile to my face. Living in
the Avalon leaves little room for plants. When I had a house,
my favorite thing was my herbal garden.

Lillie met me at the door in workout cloths. She said
working out was a priority. I was guided out to the sun porch,
where again flowers were planted everywhere. I said, "Lillie,
do you sit out here often?

She replied, "Every morning, which is the best time.
The birds are singing. It is almost like they know I am sad."

Lillie's husband was an accountant for a large firm for
twenty-five years. He worked out every day before work.

73

One morning while at the gym he had chest pains. His buddies called the hospital, and they sent an ambulance. Lillie made it to the hospital within minutes of the call. Within two hours, he was gone. Her world as she knew it ended. All their plans for vacations and retirement had ended. The love of her life was gone.

Big changes happened within minutes. No wonder we go through so much grief. It is hard to comprehend how one person can take so much hurt in just a few short minutes. This is how it works for all of us who have lost our other half. We are ripped apart from what was our life and breath of existence in this world. Life can spin on a dime.

Lillie's husband was a very organized accountant. Because of this, her finances were in good shape. I have met so many widows who have been devastated by a financial mess, as if the loss and life changes were not enough to bear, careless planning hits a hard blow, causing more endless pain.

Friends, after a brief time, seemed to abandon her. One day she decided she would do the things she and her husband had planned. She went to a Florida condo and found old friends who were happy to see her. She is thinking of selling her home and moving permanently. She said it has been three years since her husband died, but it seems like yesterday. She does not cry as often, but when she does, it is because she remembers some silly thing or fun time they had together.

I asked if she will ever marry again. She smiled and said, "Well...there is a nice gentleman in Florida who wants me to move there. I am still talking to God about it. How do you know? Am I supposed to have butterflies as if I were young again?"

I answered, "I don't know. If I did, I would write another book."

I left Lillie with a little more hope for all of us widows. She seems happy, sure of her future. She made a list of where she wanted to be and how her life was to start again and end someday. She said she had achieved most of her goals. The journey had not been easy; however, she thinks she can control how rough the path will be for her. She said if her friends were not going to help her, "God Almighty would." Prayer helped her through the rough days, and she put action in her way up out of the grief.

I had started looking for a good Christian man. So, when I was introduced to a TV minister, I thought it certainly was of the Lord. We started talking often, and I even met his parents. He was always talking about his new songs or books he was about to write. One of the evenings we were together, he said, "I have dated a thousand women, but you are the one of the finest." His big ego was not impressive to me. I refused his calls after that bit of braggadocio and never saw him again.

Jane is off to the grocery store to buy food for just one. Sometimes she doesn't eat at all. Maybe she will eat a bowl of cereal, if that. No one wants to looks at an empty chair on the other side of the table. Her husband loved her cabbage rolls, meatloaf, and lemon pie. It has been one year now and she never wants to cook again. She goes to church on Sundays and goes home alone. Jane said she and her husband used to go out every Sunday with church friends. She misses them. Her children live too far away, and she often wishes she could go be with her husband John. She said her church does not have a widow's ministry.

I decided to go ask the church why. Come on, people. Help those like Jane and me—give us a reason to live. With eight hundred thousand new widows a year, that should tell you something. Maybe if that TV minister devoted more time to helping people like Jane, instead of dating a thousand women, he could really do some good.

Rachel visited the pharmacy often during her husband's illness. It seemed as though she needed a basket to carry all the medication home with her after each visit. The last checkup on her husband was very emotional. The doctor told Jack the cancer had spread all through his body. She gathered the children around and broke the news to them. He was loved by many, and over four hundred attended his funeral. Several months passed by since the funeral, and she went back to the pharmacy to get a prescription filled for herself. The medication was for anxiety.

Tom, the pharmacist, greeted her and asked her how she was doing. He smiled and said he lost his wife also. He invited her to dinner, and they see each other a couple of days a week. She loves to cook, and he enjoys her cooking. She says she does not think she can ever love someone again the way she loved Jack, but she likes Tom. They both enjoy traveling, biking, and good books. She thinks maybe that's all you can expect after a forty-year marriage to your college sweetheart. She says her children like Tom.

One year had passed since John's wife died. His mother and father moved to Atlanta to help him as much as he needed. Not much changed for his sons—sports as usual. One Saturday John was sitting on the bleachers watching the t-ball game for his seven-year-old son when he noticed a beautiful lady on the opposing team, sitting with a little girl. It was hard for him not to stare. When she stood and started to the concession stand, he quickly followed to get behind her in the line.

John said, "I am so sorry your team is losing."

Her reply: "Well, they are having fun anyway." She smiled.

John followed with, "Does your husband like watching your son play?"

She quickly said, "I don't have a husband." Wow! John was so excited. They moved away from the concession and continued to talk. They exchanged phone numbers, then went separately back to the game.

John called her that same evening and asked her and her children to a barbeque and swim Sunday afternoon. John's mother and father agreed to watch all the children and help with the cooking and cleanup. His parents wanted them to get to know each other.

The party worked out well. The kids had a great time. The combined ages were four, five, seven, and eight. The house was full of laughter and energy. One month later, Anna and John knew they were in love, but they realized they must have the approval of their children. All four children were happy. They were getting live-in playmates. They didn't care what their parents did. John and Anna have been married for two years, and everything seems to be working out great.

CHAPTER 6

Chess Players

*The chess board is the world, the pieces are the
phenomena of the universe, the rules of the game
are what we call the laws of Nature. The player on
the other side is hidden from us. We know that his
play is always fair, just, and patient. But also we
know, to our cost, that he never overlooks a mistake,
or makes the smallest allowance for ignorance.*
—Thomas Henry Huxley

I asked a good friend of mine who wrote *Martial Arts for the
Soul* why some individuals can slough off problems and go
on with their lives, while others cannot.

His reply: the ones who cannot move on from personal
defeats do not know how to play chess. Chess is an excellent
game, which has been around since it came from India some
fifteen hundred years ago, though some claim the Chinese
invented it. A lot of life lessons can be learned playing the
game. In order to be a good chess player, you need to know
at least four moves ahead of your time to move and what
you want to do. Just like in life, you need a plan and some

strategy to achieve what you want, which can be financial, romantic, educational, and so forth. However, there is a flip side to every coin. Things are going to stand in the way of your clever, well-thought-out scheme. In chess, the opponent seeks to disrupt your plans, while crafting his own. In chess, just as in life, we constantly have to alter our plans or devise new ones. In chess, a player whose plan is foiled must still make a move. Sometimes a player will simply move a figure because he suddenly has no new plan. In chess, this is called a zugzwang move. It means moving a piece with no purpose. This will get you beat.

An example in life: the most attractive girl in high school at a forty-year class reunion said she wanted to be a nurse since grammar school. After high school, she lived with her parents, worked all summer, and saved her money for nursing school. She gave her father her money to be put in the bank each week. In the fall, she was ready to enroll, but discovered her father had spent all her money. This was devastating on several levels. Her trust in her father was destroyed, and she had no money for college. She left home and married the first person who asked her, which ended in divorce. Later, she married again, and they had three children. Her nursing hopes disappeared.

Her ambitions ended with a devastating blow. For some individuals, this would have been nothing more than a bump in the road. If she had made it to the dean's office at her local community college, she would have received a Pell Grant, been placed on work-study, and perhaps given one of the school grants that go begging each year. She would have received more money than she could have hoped to earn for college.

On the way back from teaching my art class in Boca Grande, Florida, I received a call from my landlord. He wanted to rent the space next door to my gallery, but only if they could have my space also. This was a lot of pressure. I asked him to let me think about it, and on the ten-hour drive home, I prayed and thought. I realized I love teaching more than the responsibility of the gallery. So this would allow me to travel and teach. I started feeling better about my decision to say yes. Maybe the Lord had me in my gallery for that season of grief to keep me busy, but now I am so excited for the new chapter of my life that will be starting soon. I thought about what my psychology friend said and realized I am one of the chess players in life.

I packed my gallery to move it into storage. I reflected back on when I started to renovate the space. I remembered the tears I shed when I was physically tired doing things Cliff usually did for me, like framing my paintings and hanging them. I shed tears again while taking the paintings down. The gallery is now an empty space, another chapter closed, but like Scarlett O'Hara said, tomorrow is another day. I am ready for what God has in mind.

It has been said time heals all wounds. I do not agree. The wounds remain, and in time the mind, protecting its sanity, covers them with scar tissue and the pain lessens, but it is never gone.

I was invited to dinner by a couple who have been married for ten years. Their story was one of my favorites. Mike was sixty-eight and Janis sixty-seven. They lived in the same neighborhood and went to the same high school in a small town in Ohio. They were sweethearts all through high school and decided to marry someday.

Mike went to Ohio State, but Jan went to Indiana University. She joined a sorority and enjoyed the parties and activities. Coming from a small town and dating the same boy for years, she was ready for the fun times and meeting new friends. Mike was not interested in fraternities because he wanted to finish medical school as soon as possible. Jan soon became interested in dating other guys. She informed Mike maybe they should date other people to make sure they were right for each other. Mike had been planning to give Jan an engagement ring during the Christmas holidays, but now he wondered if he should wait. He was not feeling good about Jan wanting to date others. He questioned why they should if they loved each other.

One day Jan told Mike the awful truth: she had met a senior, and they loved each other. This seemingly casual statement broke Mike's heart. He became determined to finish college, follow in his father's footsteps, and become the doctor he and Jan had talked about.

Mike's friends went out of their way to help mend his broken heart and introduced him to a young woman who became his wife. They had two children together, then she developed breast cancer and died. His two children were in high school and ready to go to college. At forty-eight, Mike found himself a single father. He worked even harder in his father's practice to escape his grief.

Jan's marriage did not work out. She blamed herself, realizing she made a mistake almost immediately, but she was determined to stay and make it work. They had one child—a daughter. By this time, her husband was unhappy and decided to have an affair. They divorced, and she remained single for ten years, swearing she would never marry again. Still, she could not get Mike out of her mind. She thought about what a fool she had been.

Jan had a long career as a lab technician. One day while typing out a lab report, she saw a doctor's name she recognized. She was shocked. Even though she thought of him often, it never occurred to her she might actually see him again. Through the Internet, she found him. Then she discovered he lived only a few miles from her. She finally got enough nerve to call his phone, but he didn't answer. Much to her surprise, he called her back within two hours.

They decided to meet for a glass of wine at a nearby café. They both cried over stories and years of memories. Neither wanted this second chance to pass them by. They married within a few days and have been together for the past ten years.

These love stories really get to me. "Pass the tissues please."

Jan and Mike's story reminded me of my story at their younger age. I had left my high school sweetheart to experience life outside my small town. My focus was on finding new friends and having fun. I lost my way, and I paid a heavy price.

Seeing this couple at dinner made me happy, but also sad for what I had lost. But like this couple, I know I can have it again. There are so many different kinds of people in this world. As I continue talking to widows and couples, I realize more and more how we are all so different. We are different sizes and heights, and have different likes and dislikes. We do not fit in the same box. How difficult it is to find the perfect match! Are we too picky? No one is perfect. We have been so used to the same person for all those years. We will never find him or her again. Some will say they will just stay alone if they can't find the perfect spouse. Maybe they are just not ready. Here I feel like I might be preaching to a friend and myself included.

I have heard it said, if you want to meet someone, the grocery store is the best place. Tom was a widower for over a year. He wanted to make a big breakfast one morning, but his refrigerator was bare. He decided to shower, get ready for golf, but go to the grocery first.

Amy's day off is Saturday. She slept late, then headed to the grocery store. She only needed a couple of things, so she put on her running clothes and ran to the store. She only lived three blocks away.

Tom was pushing his cart around the corner of the egg department when he spotted Amy. She was looking a dozen eggs over for cracked ones when the carton slipped out of her hand. Amy began to quietly sob, then she looked up and saw Tom. She was embarrassed and quickly tried to clean up her mess. Tom pushed his cart over and said, "Don't worry, let me get someone to clean this up."

Soon an employee appeared and said, "Don't worry, this happens all the time. People want to check for broken eggs and drop the whole container."

Amy and Tom introduced themselves and started laughing. Amy felt like a klutz. Tom said, "I have an idea. Let me take you to breakfast down the street; then we won't have to worry about broken eggs.

Tom missed his golf but met a great lady. Six months later, Tom and Amy were buying their own house and starting out on a new beginning. I would not suggest you go to the grocery store, drop a dozen eggs, and wait for a prince, but you never know.

CHAPTER 7

Happiness—The Myth

Whenever Richard Cory went downtown,
We people on the pavement looked at him:
He was a gentleman from sole to crown,
Clean favored, and imperially slim.

And he was always quietly arrayed,
And he was always human when he talked:
But still he fluttered pulses when he said,
"Good morning" and he glittered when he walked.

And he was rich—yes, richer than a king—
And admirably schooled in every grace:
In fine, we thought that he was everything
To make us wish that we were in his place.

So on we worked and waited for the light,
And went without the meat, and cursed the bread;
And Richard Cory, one calm summer night,
Went home and put a bullet through his head.
                                     —E. A. Robinson(1943)

One major problem that plagues a lot of humanity is how to be happy—which brings us around to the age-old question: what is happiness? If you are looking for a simple answer, I have one. Happiness is attitude. It is not what we own or how much money we make. We can become rich in terms of what we do not need.

Is there a way out? Yes, and the answers may indeed be simple, but the answers are only the road map. The journey for solutions is harder than the answers. It does us little good to be a passive, agreeable subject. We must participate. In our society, happiness seems to be an overblown state of utopia that many people think they must achieve. Feelings of happiness are not static. They are like the stock market. They go up, go down, and go sideways. You cannot be in a constant state of happiness unless you are completely psychotic. The solution is a comfortable balance. In *The Hero With a Thousand Faces*, Joseph Campbell says that the fairytale of happily ever after cannot be taken seriously; it belongs to the never-never land of childhood. Instead, we need to answer the call to adventure, to becoming our own hero in our personal drama. Nancy did just that:

Nancy's husband has been gone three years:

> *When he passed away, I thought I would die too. I didn't. After six months I had to make a choice to live or die. I decided to live. I have always been an organized person, making plans and then proceeding. My thought was always, 'I need a plan.' I sat down in my living room chair, turned on a reading lamp, and outlined what I was*

going to do with my life. The basic thing
I wanted to do was to save myself from my
grief and then decide what I wanted to do
with the rest of my life. I outlined ten things
I needed to accomplish. This is what I wrote
for me, then I started working on each:

"1. I choose to live.
2. I choose to cry less.
3. I choose to remember the good things about my husband. He had all the fruits of the spirit: love, peace, joy, long suffering, kindness, and goodness.
4. I choose to change my life even though it is painful. It will be like trying on a pair of shoes that does not fit.
5. I will choose to be in the company of positive people, not negative people. It will be hard to make changes in friends, but sometimes it is what I need for myself.
6. I choose to search for a creative space within me and to fill it with a new me.
7. I choose to be happy, laugh as much as I can, and to bring others joy when I am in their presence.
8. I choose to donate and clean out my space for a new beginning.
9. I choose to make myself healthy again, by eating healthy and exercising.
10. I choose not to blame others for my loneliness and to do more to make myself happy."

I did all ten choices, not all at once, but slowly I checked off each of them. I was amazed when one year rolled around and, after reading the list, how far I had come. I am more happy with myself than any time in my life. I travel with friends, visit relatives, and am very content being alone.

On my trip out west, I met "Spunky" Victoria in a small town in New Mexico. Victoria owns and operates an art and collectibles shop in a very old and charming building. She paints mostly western art, very abstract with brilliant colors. She does not paint as much as she would like, because she is the only one working the gallery.

When I told her I was writing a book on widowhood, she was anxious to tell her story. She was married in California to her first husband, but after three children and eleven years of marriage, her husband had a heart attack and died. This young woman had to raise the children. Lonely and tired, she met a man she fell in love with. She said he was the love of her life. She bore him twin boys. But then again, after sixteen years of happy married life, he developed cancer and died. It seemed she had grieved most of her life.

With several children still at home, she again met another man and remarried. They had heard of Cimarron, New Mexico, from some of his friends and decided to take a chance and move from California. Upon arriving, Victoria fell in love with the little "one horse town." Her husband, not so much. But they bought a nineteen-room home and opened an art gallery in an old western-type building.

Victoria soon started her abstract western paintings with a very colorful style. Her husband began to have other feelings. He developed a dislike for the town and its distinctly western atmosphere. He wanted a more exciting life in a big city. He gave Victoria an ultimatum. She would have to choose between him and the little town. She chose Cimarron.

He left her. Once again she was going through loneliness and grieving. This time not by death but by divorce.

Victoria is thinking about selling her business and doing more of her own art. Painting is a healing thing. Victoria is eighty years old now. She says if she meets someone who can be a companion, it is all she expects and hopes for.

Victoria reminds me of my own mother. My family took my ninety-year-old mother on a cruise for her birthday. She was more like a seventy-year-old on the trip. She loved every minute of the dressing up, going to the theatre, and enjoying the food. The family enjoyed watching her, knowing this might be the last trip for her. When I tried directing her and my stepfather around, she very strongly suggested I should take care of myself, and she was perfectly capable of taking care of herself.

One evening after dinner, the family was walking through the boat when she spotted the slot machines. She asked what those people were doing. I explained, "You put the money in and sometimes, if you are lucky, you might win the jackpot." She said she wanted to play that game. No one else wanted to go in with her so I said, "Come on, Mom, I'll go with you." We purchased twenty dollars each of nickels. I knew in less than an hour our money would be gone, and we would be back in our rooms. Much to my surprise, we started winning.

At one point, we were ahead almost four hundred dollars, but then our streak ran out. It took about three hours to lose all our nickels. We laughed that whole three hours, and I count this as one of the best memories I have. I smile every time I think about it.

I believe when you love someone, giving is better than taking. I think I won the jackpot when I married Cliff. He gave me so much I had to give back or I would overflow. That's what love is. I like that feeling and would like to experience it once more in the last chapters of my life.

CHAPTER 8

Dating

If the heart of man is depress'd with cares,
The mist is dispelled when a woman appears.
—John Gay

Sixty-five-year-old Nancy told me an amusing story about dating. She met Fred online and later at a coffee shop. Fred arrived ten minutes late. He recognized her and came to the table, but with company. His son and daughter came with him. He introduced them and said they were there to make sure he didn't make a mistake.

"You have got to be kidding me!" Nancy said. They replied they just wanted to protect their father. She said she had no intent to harm him or even have coffee with him. She was outta there as soon as she could pick up her purse.

Knowing how to date is difficult. The rules have changed. It seems it was so simple years ago when we were younger. The world changed with dating sites and promises you will meet your dream date! When you do decide to meet someone, can't we just do small talk? It is hard to think of something to say for an extended time. After losing your mate, small talk is so much nonsense. Playing games is not an act I have time for or know how to handle. I had a date with a divorced man. I did not think I would do so, due to the fact it carries so much baggage. Widows are coming into a relationship carrying hurt and expectations someone will potentially change this by bringing love and joy back into their lives. A divorced male may be on guard and angry. If there are children involved, it makes it even more complicated. Maybe they won't like you. Most children of widowers are protective of their parent, yet have a desire for their parent to feel happy with a genuine person. Some are concerned about someone coming in to take their inheritance.

Occasionally this does happen. When is the time to decide their opinion matters over yours? Your children don't sleep with you, eat with you, or travel with you. You need to consider the fact you are lonely. Most children get so busy with their own lives, they simply don't have time for their parent. You need to enjoy the few good, healthy years you have left with someone who makes you happy, makes you laugh, and genuinely cares about you.

Now we come to a very important point—pictures of the mind. A lot has been made of chemistry between two people. It is true there are biochemical attractions, as well as psychological attractions, and also developmental attractions. It is the latter we need to look at.

A widow for six years, Chari was meeting her online date for dinner at a steak house in Birmingham. She and this man talked several times over a five-week period. Chari had seen Frank's picture on the dating site and thought he was attractive.

A man walked into the restaurant and looked around like he was expecting someone. Finally she stood and said, "Frank?" He said yes, and the two sat down to talk.

Chari said, "Frank, you are not five-feet-ten-inches tall." He came up to her nose in height.

Frank surged his shoulders.

Chari said, "Frank, you are not forty-eight years old."

Frank replied, "I feel young."

Chari felt like she was having dinner with her father, and she said she could not sit with such a dishonest man. She stood and walked away. But then there is the opposite outcome:

Another lady told me she had a friend who wanted to "fix" her up with a blind date. Her friend said, "You will like this guy. He has a great personality." She asked if he was good looking. Her friend said, "Well, he has a great personality! Go and check him out." The lady is forty-five years old and too young not to be dating. She said her church singles group was not the place for her because the singles are so young, and she didn't think they knew how to talk to and treat someone of her age. So she went to meet the guy at a local restaurant.

She saw two men with red shirts. She was really hoping he was the one with the red t-shirt. But the other red shirt said, "Are you Brenda?"

She wanted to say, "Brenda who?" But she said yes. She decided she could talk and have dinner, but he just didn't seem to be her type. She soon realized what her friend was talking about. They planned another date, and she has been seeing him for four months. He is funny, a financial advisor for a large company, and they are taking a working trip to California. She thinks he may be the one.

Janet is forty years old, a widow, and says she is tired of dating. Apparently she has had some bad experiences. She says each of the men she dated has had ulterior motives. They either want money, sex, or someone to take care of them. She says she doesn't enjoy this kind of company. Her husband of fifteen years wanted to take care of her. He was a kind gentleman. He has been deceased for almost two years. She thinks there is something wrong with men today. She says she is not looking for a priest, just a morally good guy. She deleted her dating site and started going back to the singles group at church. However, she is suspicious even there. She says she grew up in a wholesome town. Her father and grandfather were pastors, and her standards are high. She says all her friends are married with children with no time for a young widow. She wants someone in her life, but her job as a receptionist in an office does not give her a chance of meeting anyone on the job.

Beth told me she had been corresponding on a dating site with a man who lived nine hundred miles from Atlanta. She agreed to meet him at a restaurant in Atlanta.

Jeff arrived in town, anxious to meet Beth. He had traveled from Michigan for this one date, after only a few conversations on the email site. Beth was a little apprehensive to say the least, but she agreed to the meeting. Jeff had made the dinner date at the place of her choice. They both arrived about the same time, and found each other attractive.

As they were being seated, Beth felt awkward to be at a dinner table with a stranger. It is usually more comfortable to meet for coffee on the first date. But they started the conversation about his plane flight and the restaurant. Before the main course arrived, they knew a lot about each other, mostly about Jeff. He was the stranger on Beth's turf.

Before the meal arrived, Beth knew Jeff was not going to be her type. He had already told her he had prostate cancer and could not perform on a very personal level. This was too much information in just thirty minutes. He proceeded to tell her he had an ex-wife who was not his favorite person, and he never wanted to be in her presence again. He had been divorced for thirty-six years and had no close calls. This little bit of information told Beth a lot.

The dinner and conversation lasted two hours. Toward the end of their date, Beth urged Jeff to get back to church and go to church singles events to find what he was look-ing for. When Beth asked him what he thought that was, he pointed across the table at her and said, "You!" This was a little frightening to her.

At the end of the date, they hugged and said, "Nice meeting you."

The next day Beth sent a "Thank you" note to Jeff. He replied he had not read her profile as close as he should, and he would not make this mistake again. Beth thinks the "Christian" part might have been what he was referring to.

Beth also will never allow someone to travel that dis-tance again just for dinner. She said what she should have said was, "I don't know you, so don't do that." She said he was a nice man for someone else, but she had no intention of making his visit anything more than dinner.

Each of us has a picture of the ideal romantic person to whom we will be attracted. This "mind picture" or image occurs for a number of reasons. Perhaps when we were developing a sexual awareness of others, the movies may have made an impression, a magazine model, someone in school, or a person in church may have made an indelible imprint. However we came to our conclusion, that image is there. As a result, many potentially great partners are passed over because of early imaging. You hear people express this: "He or she is just not my type."

A beautiful brunette, winning almost every beauty contest she enters, has a great personality, is a woman most men would kill for, yet she cannot seem to get to first base with the man to whom she is attracted. Her first response is typical: "What is wrong with me?" The right answer is of course…nothing.

The problem lies within the male she has an interest in, and it may be as simple as the first big impression he had of the female persuasion having been that of a beautiful, buxom blond. It may be nothing more than hair color, a certain height, or even physical measurements. It is the picture he has in his mind, and she will never be able to figure this out unless he flat-out tells her. To top this off, he may not know himself. It is not that she does not measure up; rather, he was wired differently a long time ago.

If pushed, he might request she dye her hair, have implants, wear extra high heels, and learn to speak differently. How many women would be willing to go through this kind of change? No one, I hope. The key is finding out what picture your love interest has and what image you have. It is great if you both line up. If not, maybe you should keep searching.

Several years ago BC (Before Cliff), someone introduced me to a friend. It turned out he was a CIA agent and had many interesting stories. He invited me for an afternoon of horseback riding. He asked if I could ride, and I said, "Sure!" I had not been on a horse since I was ten years old and had ridden bareback on our farm in Indiana. I knew I could not ride, but I was sure I could look good. I pulled out my designer jeans and a cute plaid shirt, along with a western hat with a feather.

Ted picked me up in a bright, new, red pickup truck, which was very fitting for a ride to the North Georgia mountain farm. Upon arriving, I picked my horse, whose name was Sweet Millie. She looked gentle enough for a city girl. I have seen enough cowboy movies over the years to remember how to get on and off and how to say whoa. I stayed behind Ted. I didn't want him to see my lack of riding skills.

It was a beautiful day; the temperature perfect. The fall leaves were all crimson and gold this time of the season. We rode in creeks and around the mountains. The ride took about four hours. I had more trouble getting off the horse than I did getting on. I felt sore—what you call saddle sore. I thought tomorrow I would pay.

Ted suggested we go for a casual dinner at the barbecue restaurant down the mountain.

We arrived back at my house about eight o'clock. Ted had been explaining to me about self-defense. He said all women living alone should know how to defend themselves. He said, "Let me show you what I mean. Come up behind me and proceed to grab me. I will show you how to flip someone over."

I said, "Okay, I have it; let me try." He grabbed me again, I did what he told me, and flipped him on his back. I screamed, "I did it!" He was shocked as much as me. Ted slowly got up off the floor, holding the back of his pants, and started backing toward the door. He said, "I have to go, you've ripped my pants!" I said I was sorry and thanked him for the beautiful day and the lesson on self-defense on his way to his car.

Ted never called me again. I still wonder why. I liked him. I still laugh when I think of Ted and see the look on his face. I could hardly walk for a week after riding a horse for four hours, but it was worth it.

Here is a valuable tip for women: Men do not think like you think and do not see you like you see yourself. Men think in broader terms and miss fine details. They have a tendency to believe what you tell them, and they are going to think in sexual presentations. You will have to be pretty badly out of shape for them to notice, and even then they may not. If you point out all your deficiencies, real or imagined, to them, this is the image you have implanted in their skulls.

Here is a major contention: Many women want reinforcement and encouragement, especially if they are concerned with being overweight, getting older, or losing some of their physical attributes. They need to seek help for these insecurities from other women. Women are good at telling each other how good they look, or how a certain style makes them look thinner, younger, cuter. Don't try to get this out of a male.

Most males, if you say you are fat, then you are fat. They may say, "Oh no! You look as good as you ever did." You are too late. Couch everything in positive terms. Men are visual. You need to paint them a picture. Tell them what to think about you.

Never, and I repeat, never, say to a male, "Do you think this dress helps to cover up my weight gain?" Say this instead: "Honey, do you think this dress makes me look too sexy?"

"Yes!"

You are wearing a new perfume. He does not notice. You do not say, "Did you notice my new perfume?" He will say yes, but he didn't. No, what you say is: "I have on a new perfume called Passion. It's designed to create lust and desire in men." He smells it now and knows what to think.

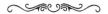

Amy had been a widow for two and a half years when she met a wonderful man through the church Bible study. She is five feet, two inches tall and very pretty. Her job keeps her busy, as she is often on call as an ER nurse. She called to cancel a date with Rob because the hospital wanted her on duty. This seemed to be happening more and more frequently lately. Rob did not want to be alone, so he called an old girlfriend for a date. The spark was lit once again, and Rob ended up dating both of them at the same time.

Amy was on her way home one evening when she decided to stop for dinner. She saw Rob with his arm around a beautiful blonde. Both girls thought they were the only one and, needless to say, Rob lost both girls that night. Amy is in a great deal of emotional pain, her confidence shaken, and swears she will never date again. She misses how faithful, loving, and kind her husband was. Rob, in her opinion, is a wolf in sheep's clothing.

If you really want to connect with a male, show him appreciation for something he is accomplishing or achieving. Women get reinforced often from other women. Males on the other hand receive few compliments. Men may say to each other, "Good speech, Joe," or "Good shot" on the basketball court or golf course, but it is surface and shallow. There is no emotional bonding. But when you give a subtle compliment, he may not respond like a female friend would and may only give a brief "Thank you." The emotional part is not what he is accustomed to, but it feels good. He has to have time to process what you said, and he will.

Melissa has been a widow for four years. Her husband died of painful pancreatic cancer at fifty-five years old. Melissa had three boys. She had been a stay-at-home mom for many years. She home-schooled twin boys, while the third was still in diapers. Before she got married, she had been engaged to a guy in college for two years. As time passed, it didn't seem to work out. Melissa broke the romance off and found her new love, married, and was very happy until her husband died.

Four months after her husband's death, she received a phone call from her old boyfriend from college. He had been divorced twice, with children from both marriages. He wanted to see her again.

After their meeting, the sparks started flying again, and they married. He was not what she remembered. He seemed to be quick to anger and very jealous. He also did not want her out of his sight. The arguments became fierce and frightening, so much so she left. She was so scared of him, she left everything she owned at his house in a remote small town.

She filed for divorce, and only saw him once after she filed the papers. He was such a controller, he had her convinced it would work out if only she would come back, just for a couple of days. She is trying to decide whether to go back or not.

This is how physical abuse starts—verbal then physical. So slow you get conditioned and do not realize you are in it. She was too quick to jump into a relationship. Even though she knew him years ago, he is not the same man today. Slow down before making a rash decision like Melissa.

The Neanderthal returns to his cave with two rabbits. Mrs. Cavewoman berates him for hunting all day and only bringing home two skinny rabbits. She hits him again with Lum (two caves down), who killed a deer so heavy it took his whole family to drag it home. His family will be eating deer steaks for a week, and Mrs. Lum will be wearing a beautiful, warm deerskin coat this winter. How many stones can you throw at a caveman?

The following day, the caveman is returning again with two rabbits. This time as he is crossing the valley, he encounters Lula, who brags on his two-rabbit kill, tells him what a good hunter he is, and how she wishes she had a cunning stalker like him to supply her with meat and rabbit fur for shoes. He makes it back to his own cave with one rabbit.

Encouraged by Lula's appreciation, he uses his tracking skills to find and kill a dangerous wild boar. His family is happy to be eating roast pork, but the wife wonders what happened to the skin!

Nancy has been a widow for two years. Her son Jim thinks it's time for her to date. She lives in Palm Beach, and her son lives in Atlanta. He requested she visit over Easter weekend. He did not tell her his real motive for wanting her to visit him: A very good friend of his father had lost his wife. He and his friend were conspiring a meeting for their parents.

Nancy is a paralegal and still works. She is sixty years old and very attractive, but also lonely. Jim arranged a meeting at a local restaurant for his mother and his friend's father. When Jim finally told his mother what to expect, she started to get nauseated. She was unsure of her son's motives. Was he tired of worrying about her and wanted someone else to take over?

She arrived fifteen minutes late because she was not used to the Atlanta traffic. She approached the table. Her son stood to hug her and proceeded to introduce her. The first impression is always so important at the first meeting. The gentleman was well-dressed, polite but quiet. It seemed Nancy did all the talking by asking questions. She guessed he was in his late seventies. She had not thought about dating someone this much older. Her first thought was how to tell her son she was not interested. After all, the man is the father of her son's best friend, but it's her life, and she does not want to get involved just because she feels guilty. Some people don't show their age. Some older individuals are full of spark and energy, but some at seventy seem ninety. After the meal, they shook hands. She knew she would never see him again.

That evening, Jim called, "Isn't he a nice man, mom?" She thanked him, then added he was too old for her. She decided right then to never again let her son plan a meeting for her. On the way back to Palm Beach, Nancy made the decision to be more aggressive on her own. It would be her decision from now on.

I am really amazed at the dating scene. My hairdresser, a very well-known lady in Buckhead, Georgia, told me a story while she was cutting my hair. Several other clients heard her roaring with laughter.

She had a recent date with someone she met on an online dating site. His profile looked interesting. She agreed to be picked up at her home for dinner. The gentleman was a New York native. He arrived on time, but honked his horn in front of her home. She thought this cannot be happening.

She opened the front door and looked straight at him, then started to walk back in. He rolled down his window and shouted, "Are you ready?" She pointed to the steps for him to come to the door. The man got out of his car and said, "What?"

She explained, "In Atlanta, men do not blow their horns for women to come out to their car. Are you sure you want to go out with me?" My hairdresser is a beautiful woman; of course he did. He even opened the car door for her. They proceeded to dinner. After a few glasses of wine, he wanted to dance. There was no dance floor, but they did try to dance. He said he was six feet, but it turned out he was the same height as my hairdresser, and when he tried to do the turn with his arm over her head, he almost decapitated her. Some men do lie, and my hairdresser will never see him again.

Gab (short for Gabriel) met me at a coffee shop today. This interview appointment came from one of my art students. He guaranteed this story would bring me to tears. I said, "I don't think so. This hasn't been an easy job; I've heard a lot of sad stories." My first impression of Gab was a startling one; he was tall, handsome, and very polite. I was wondering what kind of story he would have for me.

He grabbed my hand, shook it, and held it for a few minutes. "So glad to meet you and tell you my story," he began. The gentleness in his eyes was very apparent. Gab lost his wife one year ago. He is seventy and ready to retire. He is the CEO of a large company, and this is his story.

His wife was driving home from a business meeting with clients but did not make it. A car crash took her life. A call came to his house about nine o'clock. Gab rushed to the hospital, but did not make it in time. She died because of too many injuries. Gab's life seemed to stop. They had been married for thirty years, with no children to console him. Neither he nor his wife had many friends due to both their busy schedules. He said his life looked like a dead-end street.

He looked at me with tears in his eyes and said, "What do I do from here? I haven't dated, and I can't even imagine anyone else in my life."

I was thinking, how do I comfort someone like this? My heart ached for him. I suggested a grieving group. I had just received a phone number that day from a friend. So I gave him the number and hoped he would go to this group. He said he would. He asked me to meet him again soon after he goes to the group.

This story is not about widowhood, but a very painful loss. Jim, a young man about forty-five, was hit with a bomb three years ago. He is the father of two young boys. One afternoon, he came home from work and his wife met him at the door. She exclaimed, "I want a divorce and I want it now. I am tired of spending my life doing nothing but running after kids all day long. They are driving me crazy. I am tired of you, tired of this humdrum existence with no time for me."

Jim's legs were suddenly weak and trembling. He sat down, his head in his hands. He tried to absorb what his wife was saying. He thought they were happy. Finally he looked up and practically screamed, "Why!"

She told him again, she just wanted out. She turned and went into the back bedroom. Returning, she had with her two large bags packed and ready to go. Apparently she had been planning this for some time. She walked out the door without even saying goodbye to their two sons.

Jim sat in silence, in shock. He could not move for hours. He did not know what he could do. How could he raise two boys by himself? How could he manage work, school, the boys' sports practice and games? How could he make it without Sue? He was a lost man.

Finally, he decided to call his mother in Florida. She also was shocked. But recovering quickly, she said she and his father would be at his house the next morning.

When Jim's parents arrived, they sat in the living room and cried. This was just too much. But then together, they began to reason a way out. His mother said they would take care of the children and not to worry. Jim started to feel a little better. The two boys came into the room, and Jim hugged them both for a long time. He did not want to cry in front of them. All they understood was their mother was gone and not coming back. He put them to work helping their grandmother prepare dinner.

The next day, Jim could not go to work. He sat on the back porch all day, trying to process what was happening to his life. His parents returned in the evening. The two boys were delighted. Granddad played games with them, and their grandmother made cookies and homemade ice cream.

After the rest of the family retired to bed, Jim and his mother talked late into the night. She wanted to know what had happened. He had no answers. All he knew was his wife had screamed at him that she just wanted out. She had told him to keep the kids and the house; she didn't want anything. However, she did take two thousand dollars from their checking account. He had no idea where she went.

A few days later, she called and wanted a quick divorce. She told him to pick the lawyer, since she wasn't asking for anything. In four weeks, it was over. John went to a motel the day of the divorce. He wanted time to be alone and cry. He vowed the boys would never see him cry. Finally, when he walked out of the motel, he accepted it was over with Sue. Done. He decided on a new life, and it started right then. His whole life would be his boys.

The last report on Sue came from friends. She had moved out of town. The biggest shock: she had been having an affair with one of Jim's employees, which was another stab in the heart.

Remember the old Russian fable of the scorpion and the frog? If you are dealing with someone who has a compulsion problem, such as drug abuse, gambling, or alcohol, or has the attitude of "My way or the highway," watch out!

There once was a frog sitting on the bank of a creek. He was a happy old toad. He had plenty of flies to eat; just stuck out his tongue, and pulled them right into his mouth. The sun was warm and comfortable and plenty of lady frogs around. All was right in his world.

Along came a scorpion who looked at the creek and then at the frog. He did not ask but demanded, "I want to go to the other side of this creek, but I cannot swim. You are big, and you can swim. Let me get on your back and you can carry me across to the other side."

The frog quickly said, "No."

The scorpion, taken aback, replied, "Why not?"

The frog answered, "You are a scorpion. If I let you on my back, when we are in the middle of the stream, you will sting me. It will paralyze me, and I will drown."

The scorpion sneered and with a very degrading tone said, "That makes no sense whatsoever. If I sting you and you drown, I can't swim, so I will drown also."

Well, the slow-thinking old frog could not counter this well-said argument. Besides, he wanted to please the scorpion, so he let him crawl onto his back.

They were halfway across the creek, and everything seemed fine. Suddenly the scorpion stuck his stinger into the frog's back and released a full load of poison.

The frog was horror struck. He could feel the loss of control of his legs. Before he went under the water for good, he looked at the scorpion and with a quivering voice asked, "Why?"

The scorpion replied, "That is just the way I am."

Some people cannot seem to help destroying themselves and those who try to help them.

CHAPTER 9

Paradise Regained

How a little love and good company improves a woman!
—George Farquhar

Liz has been a widow for one and a half years with two grown children and one grandchild. She had no intentions of being on a dating site. She was flying to New York to visit her brother, because she had not seen him since her husband's funeral. Before she left for her trip, she bought new clothes and had her hair and nails done. She wanted to look good in New York. On boarding the flight, a man stood to let her sit in her middle seat. He was handsome, dressed in a sports coat and tie, which was unusual for a traveler. He introduced himself, and she explained her visit to New York. It turned out he was a widower too, going to New York for business. He asked if he could take her to a play, for which he had two tickets. They discovered they had mutual friends in Atlanta, and lived forty-five minutes from each other in the city. She agreed to go to the play. They've been dating for six months, and she thinks it may be a match.

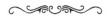

John was anxious to meet Betty Jane after three years of being a widower. He had met no one he was interested in during this time. He had tried the church singles group but without luck. John was slightly overweight and tried but could not get the weight off. Betty Jane's profile described her as a vivacious person, extremely active in church functions. John liked this. He was on the board of his church and a Sunday school teacher. He was nervous, wondering if she would like him.

As he rounded the corner of the deli, he saw her. He knew it was her as soon as he saw those beautiful blue eyes and a smile that lit up the room. He gave her a friendly hug, and they proceeded to their table. John had a good sense of humor and kept her laughing. By the way, a sense of humor is high on the list of desirable characteristics women look for in men. Their lunch lasted for two hours. It seemed like ten minutes to John. Both wanted it to go on forever.

As I talked to this couple, I could see the love they had for each other. They married after four months. You can have love again.

Rita was running late one morning. She was on her way to see her doctor, and then she had several errands. She had not been sleeping well. She wanted her doctor to give her something to help her relax. Rita had to wait thirty extra minutes for her appointment—this threw her even later.

Instead of medication, the doctor gave her some advice. He wanted her to walk every day, perhaps take up yoga, then, drink hot herbal tea before bed. He asked her to try this for two weeks, then he would consider a prescription.

After leaving the doctor's office, Rita stopped at the grocery store, a job she'd hated ever since her husband died over a year ago. Buying food for one person was hard. She did not like cooking and eating alone. She arrived at the checkout counter and discovered in her morning rush she had left her credit cards at home. Thinking back, she realized when she changed her purse to match her shoes, she forgot to put her card holder in the new purse. She was embarrassed. There was nothing to do except return home for her cards and leave the groceries.

When she sat down in her car, a new problem arose. The car was low on gas. Now she was afraid she might not make it home and back to a gas station. She was becoming more agitated by the minute. With no money and no credit cards, she could be in real trouble.

She was so disturbed as she backed out of the parking space, she hit the bumper of the car next to her. This was more than she could take. She started crying. Tears streamed down her face. Makeup merged into two tiny ribbons down her cheeks.

The gentleman whose car she hit tried to console her by telling her it was okay and there was no real damage. But Rita couldn't stop crying. Finally he put his arm around her and helped her move her car. Then he offered to take her over to a coffee shop. He said, "If anyone ever needed a cup of coffee, it's you."

They talked for at least an hour. Before he left her, Jim put gas in her car and asked her for a dinner date the next evening. This turned into a beautiful romance, and they married later in the year. You never know who you might *run into*.

I met a man who said he would give me the story of his new life. He lost his wife six years ago from a rare blood disease. After her long illness and eventual death, her husband Sam moved in with his elderly mother. Her home was large, around ten thousand square feet. This gave him room for his personal things. Sam was able to make this change in his life because his son, an only child, was forty-five and living in California with his wife and two daughters.

Sam had been a physician for many years. Retirement was not easy for him. He loved being a doctor and helping people. He and his wife Ellen had plans for travel and taking walking trips around the world. When his wife became sick, it was hard being a doctor and unable to help her. They had many talks about what he should do after her death. She wanted him to go on with his life, marry again, and travel like they had planned. She told him he deserved to do all those things, since he had worked all those years helping others. Sam thought her words were meant to comfort him. He'd loved her for forty-five years and had been faithful to her. Ellen was always there for him during his late hours and calls in the middle of the night, and she grieved with him when he lost a patient. They were the best of friends.

But his mother needed him now. After a year of caring for her, he realized he needed help. He was lonely and needed some rest and time away. So he hired one of the best nurses he knew to stay with his mother. It turned out the mother was happy to see her son leave for a break. She even admitted to him she knew she was a handful.

Sam arranged a tour of Ireland. He met his group at the airport for the departure flight. As he started talking with members of the group, he noticed a lady who seemed to be alone and a little shy. He introduced himself as a widower on his first trip without his wife. She smiled and said, "Me too."

When they boarded the plane, Sam arranged with a gentleman to exchange seats with his new friend Amy, so they could sit together. Amy admitted to being very frightened to travel alone, but knew she had to start somewhere. It had been a hard year without her husband. She said he decided the grass was greener with one of his long-time employees and asked her for a divorce on Christmas day. They had no children, so life alone was a dreaded nightmare. She told Sam she couldn't believe she was telling a total stranger her life history, especially the bad part. But things became lighter between them. They talked, laughed, and became friends. Sam found himself holding hands with her and going for private dinners. They even prolonged their tour for one extra week. Sam fell in love, and it was not a one-way street.

Sam and Amy went back, found a home close to his mother, and kept the private nurse for her. Amy likes to travel as much as Sam. They work out every day together to keep in shape for their walking tours. Sam asked me if I thought Ellen planned this for him. I smiled and said, "Maybe."

Today is Mother's Day. As I reflect on my own mother on this special day, I think about how many will be grieving the loss of a wife and mother today. Sometimes when children are grieving over their mothers, it is hard to see, as in the following:

This next interview brought me to this special story. Jon and his young daughter met me for lunch. I was surprised Jon brought his daughter, but after meeting her, I was impressed with her maturity. She had been a rock for her father. Maria was fourteen years old, a tall beauty. Jon says she was the picture of her beautiful mother. Her mother was Italian with dark hair and brown eyes. They brought a photo of her. I agreed Maria was a mirror image of her mother.

Cancer is a wicked disease. It took two years to finally take their angel, wife, and mother. Maria began telling the wonderful things about her mother. She was a fashion plate; design work was her love. It showed in every part of her life: decorating their home, Italian cooking, dressing with a flair. She helped at school whenever needed, which included helping the cheerleaders, and she had been very involved in her church, working with families with special needs.

Maria was an only child. They wanted more children, but his wife had problems in the delivery of Maria. It ended their desire for more babies. Jon and Maria held hands, one on top of the other, during our talk. They had not gone to any type of grief counseling, but seemed to be working through their loss together.

It had been two years since the death of their loved one, but with their large Italian family, their life was full. An aunt had stepped in to become a second mom to Maria. I believed this was why Maria was doing well. Her aunt was very close to her sister. There was two years' difference in their ages, and they looked very much alike. The aunt takes Maria shopping and was teaching her to cook and dance. I thought this was what families should do to help each other. It made me wish I was Italian. Maria and Jon have taken over helping families in need, which was dear to Maria's mother.

Jon and Maria will visit more family in Italy this summer. Jon does not want Maria to forget her roots. I did not ask Jon about a future relationship. It did not seem to be the time. I don't think he will be ready for someone for a while. He is only forty-two and very handsome, so I am sure he will find another mate when the time is right.

CHAPTER 10

Protect Yourself

Don't waste any time mourning—Organize!
—Joe Hill

Talking with Anna, a young, thirty-eight-year-old widow with three children, was an eye opener. Her chances of finding a young man willing to take on three children and a widow was slim. Where does she begin? A dating site asked for a profile; does she say widow with three children? With encouragement from three friends, Anna decided to try anyway. The first week was horrifying. Most of the responses were from seventy-year-old men, old enough to be her father but willing to take children. She did get response from a forty-year-old man who had *never* been married. He did not mind her children. She decided to have coffee with him. After getting his last name, she Googled him and did a criminal check. He had been arrested for child pornography. She became disgusted and deleted her entire profile. She gave up and decided God would have to drop someone on her doorstep for her to find love again. She decided to continue teaching school and being the best mother she could. Maybe someday she might meet another young widower with children who would understand her.

There are many personality types you should stay away from. Don't get too involved until you give the relationship time for you to understand the individual character of the person you are interested in. Don't marry then find out. Take Betty for example:

Betty could not believe her luck. She was marrying a dentist. Her whole family was proud of her. Almost immediately her dream turned sour. Betty was quiet and retiring. Her husband began to berate her, finding fault with her every day. Apparently he chose to marry her to have someone to bully.

It got to the point every time she heard his car in the driveway, her legs began to tremble, and she had to sit down. Like a drill sergeant, he walked through the house and listed problems: dust on furniture, clothes that were not folded to his satisfaction, or a dinner that didn't taste right.

He brought his wife to see a hypnotist. He said he wanted to see if he could help his crazy wife. The dentist left his wife for her session.

At first Betty was too ashamed to look up, but finally she shyly asked, "Do you think you can help me?"

The hypnotist replied, "I believe I can."

After putting Betty in a trance, he implanted in her unconscious mind this thought: "In your mind's eye, I want you to see a large glass box hanging just above your head. When someone starts to say anything bad to you, simply reach up with both hands and pull the box all the way to the ground. The box is clear, and you can see through it, but you will not be able to hear anything outside the box."

A few days later, the doctor returned to the hypnotist's office. He was clearly upset and mad. "What did you do to my crazy wife? Every time I start to correct her, she does the weirdest thing. She reaches above her head with both hands, then bends down and touches the floor. She straightens up with a goofy look on her face and does not hear a thing I say."

The hypnotist may have solved the wife's problem, but he gave the dentist a huge one.

One personality you definitely want to drop immediately is the psychopathic kind. Now don't be too quick to just slough this off. Psychopaths are one of the hardest to spot. First, they are not mentally ill. They simply do not have an adequate conscience, which results in poor moral development. In our society, this is a very common personality defect. Probably about one in five have this problem to a more or less degree. They are usually very intelligent; however, they are impulsive and do things they do not plan out. Sounds good, so they do it. As a result, they are extremely irresponsible and egocentric. They want what they want, and they want it now.

When you first meet this personality, you will be drawn to him or her. They are thrill seekers and take chances others will shy away from. Many times they are looked up to and even imitated. They have the tremendous ability to put up a good front to impress and exploit others. One psychologist said if he is really impressed with someone after he has known them for only a few minutes, it is a real red flag for him.

The initial reaction is you want to know more about this fascinating individual. To say they are intriguing is an understatement. Many times this individual is not only impressive but unusually striking in physical appearance as well. I think much of it is they are cunning and understand what appeals to others, so they know how to dress or apply makeup to impress people. They understand you a lot more than you understand them.

One young woman looked and dressed the part of a movie starlet. The effect she had on the male world where she worked was devastating. A young man with a promising future at the company fell madly in love with her. On the second date, they were engaged. She told him what he wanted to hear and made him feel like Tarzan. But something did not quite click. He followed her one night after work and was devastated when she met another man at a motel. Some friends discovered him in time before he committed suicide. She, on the other hand, went on to the next conquest.

Psychopaths are hard to detect in their deceit, because they do not feel guilty and don't have feelings of anxiety. Most think they are too smart to get caught.

It is easy to fall in love with this personality type. Remember, they understand you better than you understand them. They know what you are looking for, what you need, and they can offer a forever love, a permanent playmate, and best friend. You think this is the way they really are, but it is transitory. Most people who marry psychopaths remember when life was great and think it can be that way again, especially with them promising to change and always asking for another chance. Plus, while psychopaths may not feel guilt, they do not hesitate to heap guilt on others. They are great at subtle hints of things you should not have done to them! A spouse will go through life trying to figure out just what they did to deserve such treatment. This is the main key. If you are in a relationship gone sour, and for the life of you, you can't figure where you went wrong, then it probably is not you. What should you do? Quite frankly, run like hell! Run like the devil is after you because he probably is.

Donna made this tremendous mistake recently, and she is paying for it big time. It is going to take her years to recover, if she can, because of the anger and humiliation she feels.

Donna is the single mother of two teenage girls. She worked unselfishly for twelve years to provide for her family. She had no time for dates or to think about herself. She is a dark-haired beauty. One day she met her prince. He was tall, six-foot-four, dark, handsome, and looks like he belongs on a romance novel cover with his shirt unbuttoned. Like a character out of love story, he told her what she yearned to hear. She felt so special. He understood her so well, but she could have fallen in love with him on his looks alone. He was absolutely perfect.

Donna's two girls had told their mother to meet someone, because they soon would leave for college, then a career. Everything seemed right. The smooth-talking, handsome man insisted Donna go with him back eighteen-hundred miles to see where he lived and to meet his family. He bought her the airline ticket. He had already met her family, and everyone was impressed with him, except her mother. But maybe she was being too overprotective.

Her house had been on the real estate market and had just sold. She felt all the stars had lined up, and this must be divinely ordered. Her dreamboat said he did not drink and was heavily involved in church work. She checked him out on Facebook, and he had many friends who seemed to love him. Much to the concern of her mother, she left for that long trip.

That very weekend, she called back to her family in Atlanta to say she was married. She was deliriously happy. He had taken her to Las Vegas to be married. Everyone had very mixed emotions, but had to accept it. She flew back to

Atlanta to pack her belongings and prepare for her move. He came to Atlanta the next day and helped her pack her things into a U-Haul truck. She checked all her money out of the bank and closed her account.

Two weeks later she called, crying and saying, "This is terrible!" It turns out, he was a closet alcoholic and drank well into the night. He was already verbally abusive. He was starting to become violent. Once in a rage of temper, he threw her across the room, damaging her arm. She was scared of him.

With bruises and very hurt emotionally, she made the decision to drive the eighteen-hundred miles back to Atlanta, leaving her furniture. She is back in Atlanta and starting over, as if she were single. She had the marriage annulled, but he kept her furniture and the money she had from selling her house. Not only did he take everything she had, but also took her trust and turned her life upside down. The big question: will she ever be able to trust another man again?

Dating sites have some success stories, but on the other hand how many end up in destruction? Donna is now trying to put her life back together. She is looking for a job and a small apartment.

The anger she feels is so damaging. In many cases like this, the victim blames themselves. She blames herself for trusting him. He took more than her money and furniture. He took something so precious: the love she had stored up for someone special. She wakes up at night, terrified over the scary and dangerous physical abuse. She is afraid of what would have happened to her if she had stayed.

My advice: if you find yourself being verbally or physically abused, leave right then and do not blame yourself. These personality types are so smart and understand you so well, you don't have a chance. Until they get you committed, they are the most wonderful, caring person you will ever meet. They can then turn on you on a dime. They are capable of hurting you. Save yourself!

I am going to throw out a few more personality types to avoid. It may take several dates before their true nature shines through. Narcissistic people are totally self-focused and have no empathy for anyone else. The trait which gives them away, even in the beginning of a relationship, is their grandiosity. Their ideas and schemes have no bounds and they are all centered on how great they are. They may offer for you to tag along, but they have no interest in what you want to be or do. You are window dressing. If you cease to massage their inflated ego structure on the scale they need, then you are history.

Obsessive people are always striving for perfection. They will be stubborn, dictatorial, and rigid, always insisting they are right. You will be fine if you always give in. You may have to kiss a lot of frogs before you find your prince.

JoAnn had an appointment at eleven o'clock Saturday morning to meet her mystery date at a local coffee shop. She was excited to meet this guy. His profile said he was addicted to working out, from which she gathered he was a bit of an exercise freak and probably very physically fit.

She arrived early to have a good look when he came through the coffee shop door. He arrived on time. He was a large, tall man dressed in shorts and a very wet tank top. He was over the line for her. She told me, "I think he sprayed his shirt before arriving. It didn't look like perspiration. His hair was wet. He came to my table and asked if I were JoAnn. I said, 'No. But I do know her and I think she just went out that door.' I pointed to a side door. I know I lied but he lied too."

As she walked back to her car, she vowed never to do this again.

I said, "But JoAnn, he was just trying to be a cool guy. You should have met him anyway." She said she might have liked him if he had not shown up in a wet shirt and shorts. First impressions do make a difference.

I was excited to meet another man recently to get his story. I was given his number from a lady at the makeup counter where I shop. I find it amazing how many people want to know more on the subject of widowhood. I arrived at eleven o'clock at a local café. A neatly dressed gentleman came to my table and asked if I was Bonnie. We were there early enough to beat the crowd. We greeted each other with a handshake. We immediately ordered coffee. While waiting, we discussed the weather and how it looked like rain. When coffee arrived, he poured in cream then piled in sugar, more sugar, and more sugar. I said a stupid thing, "Wow, you like a lot of sugar."

He replied, "Darling, I do love my sugar and plenty of it, especially depending on where the sugar is coming from."

I am sure my face turned red. I changed the subject. "How long have you been a widower? Tell me about your loss."

He said, "Oh no, I'm not a widower. I've been married and divorced four times. I would have liked to have been called a widower a few times. That would have solved a lot of problems for me."

I asked him how long he had been divorced from his last wife. He said three months and he was moving on. Then he said, "I don't have any rug rats, thank God. I would hate to have that hanging over me, and I probably would have had to pay child support. I also have two bull dogs that will tear up anyone who gets near me." I was thinking this might be a set-up from an ex-wife at the makeup counter. I couldn't help it, I blurted out, "I need to go to the ladies room." Lunch had not been ordered, so I could escape. I headed for the front door as fast as I could. I didn't know if I should laugh or cry. I would have stayed if I could have helped him, but if four wives could not help him, I doubt anything I said would have made a dent. The sad part is, he is out there looking for wife number five.

Don't forget the story of the scorpion and frog.

I enjoy walking in the Avalon early in the morning. I love that time of the day, when no one is around except the window washer and street cleaner. The only noise is the street blower and my footsteps. I greet my "Good morning, friends," the window washers. They know my dog Bella by name, but they don't know mine. No hugs, no "Good morning, sweetheart, here's our coffee." I miss the mornings with Cliff the most. It was always the best part of my day.

As I turn the corner to the coffee shop, Bella pulls a little harder on her leash. Dogs are allowed in the coffee shop, and everyone talks to her. This is where she gets her treat. While walking, I reflected on my day yesterday and my talk with the man I thought was a widower but was shocked to find he had been divorced four times. That short conversation was a disappointment and a bad ending to a beautiful day.

Lynn started her interview like a number of women I talked with by saying, "My story is not very exciting." She married her high school sweetheart. He received a football scholarship to play at the University of Florida. She was so excited, she planned to go to Florida State University with one of her best friends. A few weeks after he signed with Florida to play football, he got drafted to play baseball with the Cleveland Indians. He made the decision to play baseball. After a few years, he was playing in Reno, Nevada. His parents were going to drive across the country to see him play.

"He called them and asked for them to bring me, and we would get married." Lynn had no idea he was planning their wedding. Instead of riding with his parents, he sent her a plane ticket. They were married in a little wedding chapel across the street from the court house. She had a great time while he played ball, but soon, he decided he wanted to return home and enroll in college.

Lynn said she worked full-time, and her husband attended classes at the University of Florida. He received his degree in pharmacy. Life was great. They started their family, and both of their families were thrilled they were married.

"We had a daughter named Kathy, followed by twin boys." Eleven years later she was pregnant again. It was not long after their daughter Kathy was born, Bill started having trouble with his blood pressure. He was soon diagnosed with polycystic kidney disease. On Christmas day 2000, he got a call for a kidney transplant. He received a perfect kidney and had many more healthy years.

Bill was able to see his grandchildren born. He was a wonderful granddad and the kids all called him B. He became active in their church. He was so grateful to be alive. He went through many surgeries, and in the end at sixty-seven, he was diagnosed with stage-four melanoma. He died one week later.

"The next few days were a blur for me." Many of her friends and family took care of things she found hard to do. She felt numb. She couldn't really accept Bill wasn't coming back. Six months later she wanted to leave and not tell anyone where she was going. She drove away but did not get far before she turned the car around and went back home.

Lynn wrote down the names of several psychologists on a piece of paper. She picked one and saw him for three years. She didn't know who she was without Bill. They had been together since she was fifteen. She recognized part of her died, but she said she finally found herself. One day she realized if she was worthy of Bill loving her, she must not be so bad. She renewed her relationship with God, who she had been angry with for a long time.

She also renewed an old relationship. She said a wonderful friend she had not seen in years called her. "Bonnie Flood was writing a book and wanted my story." Lynn said she became so engaged in telling what had happened to her, she realized she could have fun again.

She started smiling and said she had the most beautiful painting of an angel on her wall. She felt it was her Bill. She purchased the painting in an art gallery in Florida. One day she looked at the artist's name, and it was painted by Bonnie Flood. Small world!

CHAPTER 11

Life is the Great Adventure

A flower grew where none could grow,
an impossibly to the Earth.
Trodden down by immense wind and
stepped on by a giant foot
But then the sun came and strength regained
dried the petals with cooking pain
It stood a little and then some more
soon was straight and tall
It's arms outstretched up to the sky,
it's beauty seen by every eye
I'm here I survived, stronger than ever
The sun and rain helped me to grow
I have the Son
I'm here, and I know from whence
My strength did come.

—Patty Staggs (1979)

A very special friend wrote me poems of encouragement.
I still have those poems in my Bible. I especially love the
one above. I have not seen this friend in years. She is on my

Facebook, but if we saw each other today, we could not stop talking. Most of the people I knew in my Bible study group are on my Facebook page. I am so grateful for the prayers and strength I received from my Bible study group.

> *Rain comes when the clouds can no longer hold the rain.*
> *Tears come when the heart can no longer hold the pain.*

I hope this does not come as too big of a shock, but you are different. Like a snowflake, there is not another you anywhere. You are an original. One of the worst advertisements I have heard promoted young people to be part of an original crowd. There is an oxymoron for you! We need to celebrate our differences, rather than be molded into some common denominator.

Sometimes we wish we could be someone else or at least have what they have. This is invalid thinking. We immediately think how we would change what this person does, which invalidates the desire to be someone else or have their exact possessions. If you are an American citizen, you are better off economically than over ninety percent of this poverty-stricken world, no matter your circumstances. Yet current research indicates that America ranks low in happiness compared with other countries. Remember, happiness is nothing more than attitude, and it comes and goes depending on our mood. That attitude is different for each one of us. Happiness means something different to a western hermit than to a New York socialite, different for a multimillionaire CEO than the hourly wage earner in his plant, different for the fired-up evangelist than the college football coach.

Most new situations produce anxiety. The hero in a drama is summoned to venture out of his or her comfort zone to situations they have not encountered before. The neurotic, on the other hand, suffers from an excessive check on his impulsive nature. Therefore, he has trouble solving the problems or tasks life places before him. In other words, the neurotic individual simply thinks too much. Too much introspection is not good for us. It causes us to have negative feelings about ourselves.

Since we are social animals, all of us seek and need the friendship of others. Friendship means something different to each of us, depending on how we see ourselves, our situation, our drama, and our quest. Consider Tom's situation:

It was spring break. Tom was taking his teenage son and daughter to Orange Beach. Tom's wife passed away the year before about this same time, and he wanted a change of scenery. The kids were excited and had been planning for weeks for this special trip.

Tom finds trying to be mother and father to two teenagers can be exhausting. He needed this trip as much for him as for his kids. His wife had been ill for a year and a half. She was bedridden for six months. He was a college student with a full-time job. With exams at school and all the stress of his sick wife, taking care of the kids was overwhelming.

Now they were at the beach surfing, eating seafood, sunbathing, and enjoying the nightlife. This time at the beach was giving Tom a chance to be alone with his children and bond with them.

One day Tom found himself alone having a quiet lunch, with the teens off at the beach, and he finally broke down and cried. He had not allowed himself this outpouring of emotion when his children could see him.

A couple in the restaurant saw him and came over to his table to ask if he was okay. He simply said, "No." The couple sat down, one on each side of him. Tom blurted out his life's story and the reason for this trip.

It turns out the man was a pastor on vacation with his wife. They sat and talked for several hours. Tom said he felt like he had been to a counseling session, and a weight seemed to be lifted from his shoulders. Tom's life changed that day because of two sensitive strangers. The rest of the week he said he felt light and free with a hope for the future. When he returned home, he was ready for a new beginning and became a better father for his children.

Two of my best friends and I were going to lunch one day. The silence in the car was suddenly broken by my friend in the backseat. "Do you know why the three of us are such good friends?" It was obvious from the expression on my other friend's face and mine we did not have a clue. The answer from the backseat: "It's because none of us has anything the other would have."

I have reflected on this statement many times. Maybe this is one of the keys to true friendship—no envy. Envy is such a deterrent to human happiness it is condemned as one of the seven deadly sins. In a modern, materialistic world, it is a hard concept to combat. Creating envy in others with lots of things, is a shallow measurement of success and will not win true friendships.

I seem to enjoy those friends who I can't seem to insult. They don't carry their feelings on their sleeves and don't allow me to go unchecked. I must admit, they do have a rather cute sense of humor. I suppose if you combine my friend's theory and mine, you have friends you do not envy and have the freedom to speak your uncensored mind without social consequences, which makes for ideal friendships. We all have "Freudian slips" from time to time and wish we could take them back. It makes for a great relationship when we are not held accountable for these slips between brain and tongue. A true friend can say just about anything, and we are not offended, even when it hits a personal "weak spot." Someone we think does not like us can say the same thing and we bristle.

I closed my studio and gallery over a month ago to make room for a large spa, but now I am having second thoughts. Getting up in the mornings and looking forward to sharing my gift of teaching was so fulfilling. I miss visiting with friends who just dropped in to chat or to see my new paintings. When I started construction on the gallery after the death of my husband, it kept me exhausted, which was a good thing. I thought at the time it was helping me with my grieving, but I now think it was a false grieving. There are stages to grieving, and I think I didn't have enough time at the beginning. I filled it with work and missed some of the stages. I think in my quiet time now, I am reliving some of that. I am feeling very insecure about my future, insecure about my life in general. Who am I, and where am I going? Cliff told me to move to Avalon after his death, and after a year I would know what I wanted to do with my life. He has been gone for two years now, and I have lived in the Avalon for one year. I still don't know what the real purpose is for my life. Should I go or should I stay? I have not found the answer yet, but the Lord says, "One day at a time." The scriptures bring me strength.

The one concept I hope you have gleaned from this book is your life can turn around quickly in a good way. There are three directions: you can continue on the same path, change directions to more positive thinking, or take the turn to a deeper negative journey. It is like the football coach said of the forward pass: "One of three things will happen. Two of them are bad, and one of the two is very bad!"

I met a very pretty woman at a restaurant for an interview. Her name was Linda. Her story contained a lot of grief and so much joy. She had much more adventure and heartache than one person should have in a lifetime. Linda went through widowhood twice. The first time she was forty-five years old.

Linda and her husband were on vacation in Michigan, visiting his mother. He had grown up in his mother's house and loved the lake. Fishing was a big part of his life as a young boy, and he still enjoyed it as an adult. The morning was misty and foggy when John left the house. He may have left as early as six o'clock. When Linda woke up at eight-thirty, she looked out the bedroom window and saw the boat was gone. She heard laughter in the kitchen and smelled coffee. Her kids were watching grandma making pancakes. The laughter was a good sound. They rarely came back to Michigan these days. Their schedules were so busy; it was hard to get away.

At eleven, Linda looked at her watch. John should be back any minute. She thought he should be here spending the last day with his mother. They were going home tomorrow. Linda looked at her watch at twelve o'clock. Surely he will come back for lunch. She was really going to let him have it when he did get back!

At one o'clock, Linda started getting worried. She knew fishermen get carried away if the fish are biting, but this was getting ridiculous. When his mother said she was worried, Linda panicked. His mother suggested they call the next-door neighbor and ask him to go out in his boat and find him.

At three o'clock, the doorbell rang. It was the neighbor and a man in uniform. They found John's boat but not John. A search party was already diving and looking for him. Then the news: John had drowned.

For three years, Linda struggled with anger and guilt. She tortured herself with thoughts that if she had gotten up earlier, she could have stopped him. She sometimes thought out loud that thank God he didn't take their son Stanley, which he normally did. Probably what happened was they stayed up late playing cards, and John wanted the kids to sleep in.

Several years later one of her friends called and said her husband had a friend coming into town for a job interview and would she like to join them for dinner. Linda said she would. It had been so long since she had laughed or spent time with adults.

So was this a real date? Her next thought was she only had workout clothes, tennis shoes, and no girlie stuff. She went on a quick shopping trip with her friend, who encouraged her, saying she would help and telling her not to panic.

During dinner, Linda was thinking this felt pretty normal and really good. Bob took her home and said he would like to see her again. She was thinking she might still have a life again. Bob moved to Connecticut two weeks later. They had a whirlwind affair. She felt sixteen again. In one year, they were married.

Finding love again was such a gift. They were married for a fast thirteen years. Bob's children came once a month and spent the summers with them. Combining the kids worked out great. They all got along fine.

One day, Bob played hooky from work, deciding to take advantage of a beautiful day. He called it a perfect golf day. He thought he worked hard and deserved a play day.

About one o'clock, Linda's cellphone rang while she was at the grocery store. It was one of his golfing friends. "Linda, come right away. Bob has had a heart attack." She said she thought she was having one also. She said to this day, she doesn't know how she made it to the hospital. When she arrived, she found several friends standing outside waiting for her. From the looks on their faces, she knew she was too late. Several of her friends took her back to see him. One friend took her directly to her doctor for tranquilizers. She said she couldn't have made it without her family and friends. She kept thinking she must be having a bad dream. It would take weeks before she was able to do normal things again for herself.

She remembered thinking, "Does God hate me so much he made me a widow two times? What kind of a person deserves this?" She walked around like a zombie. It seemed like weeks. One day Linda decided enough is enough. She was not going to die. Whatever the reason God chose this path for her, she would live it. She went back to counseling. By this time, Linda knew the ropes and could have taught a counseling class of her own. It took a year, but finally Linda felt like herself again. She decided to go back to the hospital as a volunteer at the front desk. Helping others always helped her feel useful and needed.

While sitting at the front desk one morning, a gentleman walked up and asked for the room of a patient. He said a very good friend had surgery yesterday, and he wanted to visit him. Linda said, "Well, just let me walk you up there." In the elevator, she didn't waste time. By the time they got to the room, she knew he was a widower for one year, also where he lived, but she thought she would never see him again. Back at her desk, she felt a little disappointed, but soon was busy.

In about an hour, she looked up, and there he stood. "You were so kind to walk me to the room. Can you take a coffee break?"

Linda said she was thinking, "Are you kidding me? I would get a patient to watch the desk if I had to." It was perfect. In fact, she enjoyed his company so much she invited him for an Italian dinner at her house. She thought of the old adage, "The way to a man's heart is through his stomach."

They have been married for three years. He promised her he will not make her a widow for the third time. He plans to live as long as Moses.

Linda could have given up on her life and become a recluse, but she moved on each time to make her life better. We can take a lesson from Linda. I asked her at the end of our talk to tell me her secret for making it through two deaths.

She said, "It's no secret. Number one was my faith in the Lord, and second, I needed to be here for my children. It seemed everyday God gave me the strength to make it." Well that was my answer from this very strong woman. With a hug and again wiping my tears, I moved on to my next story of love the second time around.

My tears have stained my notebook. When I think I have heard it all, another story comes that tops the last one. I guess if I had not become a widow, these words would be just sad stories. I started thinking how many more widows there are than widowers. I had this vision of the great land rush in 1889—wagons all lined up, rushing to find the best piece of land. Actually it was pretty funny vision.

I am not sure why that came to my mind. A little humor helps us cope with sadness. I am not suggesting we widows line up the wagons for a rush. If we keep busy doing worthwhile things, volunteering like Linda and helping others, he may find you. Or you may find him.

Finally, remember the fun of life is the adventure. Other people in your life's drama are not the hero. The hero will meet guides, but they are only guides and not the hero.

A motorcyclist stopped to help an old cowboy whose truck had stopped running and was parked on the side of the road. When the truck couldn't be fixed, the cowboy asked for a ride back to his ranch. The biker agreed, and later after a hardy dinner at the ranch house, the two men sat in rocking chairs on the front porch, watching a golden Wyoming sunset. The old cowboy was in a talking mood and took this opportunity to tell his story.

My mother died when I was just a small kid. It was just me and my paw. He worked hard on this little ranch all his life. Never was much money, but come Saturday me and him would get in his old truck and travel all the way to Casper. It was only

*forty miles, but it seemed like another world
to a kid.*

The cowboy took a deep draw from his cigar and
enjoyed remembering:

> *On Saturdays, back in those days, they
> had a matinee movie starting at one-thirty
> at the Majestic Theater. Man, that was the
> best time of my life! They always showed
> westerns. My favorite was Roy Rogers.
> No matter what bad things happened to
> the people on the screen, in the end, here
> comes Roy, six guns a-blazing! He had the
> best-looking brace of pistols I ever saw and
> the most beautiful Palomino horse. And
> could he ride! I never saw him bounce in
> the saddle, not once. Yea, Roy never took
> nothing off nobody. He could whip any-
> body, outshoot the meanest coyote that ever
> robbed a bank or rustled a cow. He always
> saved the day.*

The tone in the voice of the old cowboy became softer.

> *When I was fourteen, my daddy died.
> He left me this ranch. Probably the worst
> thing he ever did to me. It was his dream,
> not mine. I remember how sad and lonely I
> felt that first night back here without him.
> I remember thinking, where's Roy?*

The cowboy sent a puff of smoke swirling toward the porch ceiling and then continued:

> *I never made much but never lost much. Everything just about equaled out. I had two cows die one winter and had to sell two more to pay the taxes. Again I wondered, where's Roy? But then my remaining cows had fifteen calves in the spring. Each time something had happened that just about wiped me out, I would come out here on this porch, sit in my rocker and say out loud, where's Roy? But nobody ever came galloping to save the day and make things right. But you know what I finally figured out?*

The biker shook his head but leaned forward to catch this moment of truth.

The old cowboy said it all:

> *I finally figured it out. Hell...I'm Roy!*

As a busy artist, I do not have much time for "just me." I have a friend who gave me the chance to take a trip to Northern New Mexico. Santa Fe and Taos are my favorite places to see art. I agreed to spend one week visiting in my favorite state. We rambled through art galleries in each city we visited.

If you are a woman, you cannot be in New Mexico without frequenting jewelry stores, which dazzle the eye with different shades of turquoise embedded in heavy Indian silver.

We went into a lovely shop on the main street in Taos and were greeted by a beautiful, petite, dark-haired lady with an infectious smile. It just happened we were her only customers at that moment. We started a conversation. She said she had lived in Taos for over thirty years. I mentioned the book I was writing on grief and widowhood. At that point, she wanted to know the title of the book, because she had problems in her life she was working on. The more we talked, the more she opened up. Tears began to well up in her eyes. I asked her if I could come back and get her story, and she agreed. My friend left me so I could go back alone and continue my interview.

When I returned once more, Judy was alone in her store. Sometimes fate is like that, almost as if it was planned for us to meet. As Judy shared her story, I felt every pain she went through. I felt as if I could put her name on my story.

Judy had moved to Taos over thirty years ago. She was nineteen and living in San Jose, California. Her parents owned an equipment rental business. Alex, a young, tall, handsome Hispanic man became an employee of the company. He was immediately attracted to Judy. They started dating. It was surprising her parents let her date him, because he was nine years older. He had the advantage over a naïve nineteen-year-old girl, but they were soon married. He quit his job working in her parents' company and moved her closer to his home town in New Mexico. He started a new job with Frito Lay in Farmington, New Mexico.

They bought a house, and things looked good, except her husband Alex did not want her working outside the home, so she started a small daycare business. She operated the childcare in their house. She filled her desire for children with the home business and did not have any children of her own.

Alex was always fond of alcohol, but his drinking seemed to get worse. He became verbally abusive and started pushing her around. There were days when Judy thought she could not take it anymore and wanted to go back to California to her parents, but he would say he was sorry and plead for another chance.

When he was not drinking, he had an outgoing, pleasant, likeable personality.

Slowly Judy developed into a submissive wife to keep peace. She had no friends, in order to keep him from being jealous. He wanted her attention only on him. She wanted to leave but became too weak to follow up on her plans. Alex's father was a Church of Christ minister. Judy loved and respected him. He was always kind to her. She went to his church as often as she could to keep her sanity.

Alex did not have God in his life and did not want to hear about him or want any help from the church. Alex's father kept telling Judy over and over to "Hang in there."

Alex became so obsessed with Judy's beauty, he took photos all the time to put in albums. On the other hand, when he was drinking, he would put his hands around her neck just to let her know what he could do to her if she ever left him. Judy was constantly intimidated with this kind of action. Alex's other siblings were even more dysfunctional. One brother shot and killed his partner of forty years and then shot himself.

Judy remained married for fifteen years. The verbal and physical abuse escalated. Finally, one night in a rare moment of courage, Judy blurted out, "I want a divorce."

Hostility showed in Alex's face, and he shouted back, "I am telling you, you will never make it!"

The next morning when Judy woke and Alex had left for work, she found a large knife next to her body. She became extremely frightened. When he came home that afternoon, she asked him about the knife. He refused to discuss it. She thought he was playing mind games with her to scare her and keep her from leaving.

Alex and Judy moved to Taos when he got a better job. Judy liked Taos better than Farmington and finally made the move toward the divorce. He broke down and promised her one half of all their assets. His promises never came to fruition. She received absolutely nothing, and like many women in this kind of situation, she just wanted out. She soon landed a job with a nice jewelry store. Her boss was very kind and sympathetic to her. She did not want to make waves. She just wanted safety and peace. She started going to church in Taos. She did not have a penny when she received the divorce, and having no experience working outside the home was frightening. But soon the very small jewelry store doubled sales and then tripled the money coming in. Her boss expanded the business.

Judy's boss realized the increase in sales was due to Judy, and kept raising her salary. Judy taught herself how to read the stock market reports and began investing wisely. After thirty years of working and investing, she could retire and be comfortable. She made it all on her own.

Alex remarried shortly after their divorce, quit his job, and he and his wife went on welfare. They had four children together. He developed cancer and died. Judy began to cry because she still loved him. She has not remarried and plans to move near her twin sister in Arizona after she retires. I asked her if she would ever marry again, and she said, "If God wants me to, I will."

I had a feeling we would meet again. We had a bonding which came from the depths of our souls. I felt her pain to the point of tears.

If I could have, I would have said to Judy during her trial to leave immediately when the first abuse started. I wish someone had said that to me all those years ago. It takes a long time to believe in yourself again and even more years to trust someone. Judy feels free now and very contented with her life, which consists of long hours at her job. I am hoping she will find a new love and can again experience the joy which was lost.

CHAPTER 12

Let's Get Help

*Life is not so short but there is always
time enough for courtesy.*
—Ralph Waldo Emerson

Janice is a counselor at her church, helping those who have
lost loved ones. She lost her husband and needed someone
to talk to, but her church had no department for dealing
with grief-stricken widows. She spoke with the board and
pleaded for a position to help others. She is an experienced
PA. She convinced the board she was qualified and experienced enough to know how others felt.

Her first widow was a real jolt to her. Janice felt she
was ready, but ended up in tears along with the lady she was
counseling. However, the woman came back weekly for four
months, and now she is helping. Janice's group has grown
to twenty women in six months. The ladies talk about their
troubles, feelings, and the journey to healing. Janice feels
God brought her to this position. Her prayer every night is:
"God, help me to help these women to find their purpose, to

give them hope and some joy. Guide me to show them love and compassion."

The law of attraction suggests you feel you are worthy; therefore, you send out a message you are important. If you do the opposite, you send out a different message: you are unworthy of friendship, and you may eat too much, dress sloppy, stop exercising, and treat others with disrespect. If you are spending your time and energy on thoughts of fear, worry, sadness, and guilt, you are losing out on a chance to connect with others. The more you give of yourself, the more you open the door for the good light of life to pour in. Once you start interacting with people again, you will notice miraculous things happening in your everyday life. You are becoming a chess player.

I was introduced to Justin, a gentleman in his late sixties. We agreed on a dinner interview. His wife died of breast cancer, a three-year ordeal. I asked how he had managed being alone for four years. He laughed and said, "Well, I visit the local restaurants a lot. They know me by my first name."

Justin is a good-looking man and is sharply dressed down to the shoes, designer no less. He is still a practicing lawyer and would like to find the right person to spend the rest of his life with. I asked him what he was looking for. His qualifications were: good looking, interesting, intelligent, compassionate, and in love with the Lord.

"Wow," I said, "That is some list."

He smiled a beautiful smile with his brown eyes sparkling and said, "Why not go for the gold?" He asked, "By the way, is this strictly business?" I told him for tonight, it was. Men have great expectations too. They hope they meet someone with the same goals. Justin said he had a few close calls, but they were not that compatible. When he said he enjoyed the arts and classical music, I wanted to raise my hand and say, "Hey! Me!"

I stayed professional because, after all, it was just an interview with dinner. He said it hadn't been too lonely due to his busy schedule, but the holidays and weekends are harder. He has two sons: one is a California lawyer and the other is an investment broker. He has no grandchildren yet. No dog or cat or bird. He asked if he could call me. "Strictly business of course." He said he might have more information for me later. I said I was looking forward to it.

For some reason, Annie wanted to give me her story. She began by saying she did not have much to say.

> *The first few years of widowhood, a couple friends took care of me, then I think their husbands got tired of including me. However, to be fair, I think I was rejecting them, finding them quite boring actually. My girl friends who are all married always said, 'Let me see what hubby says.' Of course I was one of those before my husband died.*
>
> *The newfound freedom of not having to check with anyone about plans is quite liberating. When I was in my sixties, sex was important, so finding someone compatible was seemingly worth the effort. However, no one lasted more than a year.*

Now in my seventies, sex and dat-
ing are not quite as important. My inter-
ests have developed and are fulfilling. My
friends, family, and grandkids fill the hole
in my heart, and life is good. I bought a
new espresso machine, and it makes my cof-
fee just perfectly.

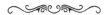

I read an article recently which said man is geared to live to be twenty-five years old. However, thanks to medical science, this may be stretched to beyond one hundred years. Many people think old age is a scene of sorrow, illness, and poverty. Everyone wants to live a long time, but no one wants to be old. Old age often comes as a surprise. It catches us unawares. We need to look at old age as a problem only we can solve. Take steps to increase your enjoyment. If you are lucky, you will have the same friends as before and do the kinds of things you enjoyed in the past. If not, find new friends, discover different things you like to do. The flip side of this coin is boredom and depression.

I got the name of another widower from the local church. Jim sits at home all day on his computer, reading the stock market and world news. He doesn't go out much, except for the grocery store. He makes hot dogs for himself and for his dog. He knows he doesn't eat right, but every now and then someone will bring him a casserole. He doesn't enjoy company anymore. He prefers to be alone with his dog. He just wants to sit and think about his wife and doesn't feel he has any purpose. He watches church on TV, but doesn't go. His house is in need of repair, but he doesn't care. His wife has been gone for two years, and he says he just doesn't care about anything anymore. He says he is ready for the Lord to come take him home because he is seventy-nine years old. He told me things are fine just the way they are, then he thanked me for calling.

There are many organizations open to you, no matter your age. You do not necessarily have to seek out grief groups. While it may be good to express your grief verbally to others, this will only go so far. Get out of the house and seek new activities. Think what brings you joy. It is different than what your neighbor enjoys. Churches offer all kinds of activities other than sitting in a pew on Sunday mornings. Local community colleges offer tuition-free courses for individuals above a certain age. You can take a college course just for the fun of it, and if you choose, you can take it for credit or noncredit. If you take it for noncredit, you do not have to take exams, and you will not receive a grade. You can learn something new just because you want the knowledge.

Many charitable and philanthropic organizations will be happy to have you as a volunteer. Helping politicians increases political power for the elderly every year. Many people once they are living alone will have more time to do things but can't find things to do. There is little to be said for just killing time. When you start gardening, taking up painting, needlework, or keeping a pet, you meet others with similar interests. Call old friends you have not heard from in years!

CHAPTER 13

What Widows Want

That best portion of a good man's life,
His little, nameless, unremembered acts
Of kindness and love.

—William Wordsworth

I have been welcomed by so many widows and widowers to tell their stories. I even received phone calls from people I did not know who heard somewhere I was writing a book and they wanted to tell their story. I will always be curious to know about the new widows. I am still not at the end of my journey. My husband has been deceased for two years. All these stories help me see myself better. I cried with these women and laughed when their stories were humorous. I hope on your healing journey you can find yourself in between the lines of this book and know you are not alone. I hope you discover your feelings are normal and real. I have come to realize with time the pain gets a little easier.

Some of the common threads I found in talking to widows involved things they do not want to hear such as "Call me if you need something," "We will have you over for dinner soon," "We will pick you up for dinner someday," or the ever-popular "We have not heard from you; you must be doing great."

A widow does not think she should have to call you. She feels she is barely able to breathe. She doesn't cook much now that her husband is gone, so take her something and take time to visit. Going out to dinner with a widow should not be a chore. If it's about paying for her meal, she will gladly go "Dutch." I know now I have more compassion and know not to say empty words. I should not say this, but you will be there someday.

In my two years, I have taken different paths, maybe a little too early, such as trying to cover the grief, working and teaching too soon. You cannot cover up your grief. Pain is pain. Trying to be strong is only a delay. We should not feel weak when we cry. We should scream, cry, and get angry. That is all normal! You and only you will know when the healing starts.

I still remember the day I decided to get up and do something. It was hard, but I went for a walk that felt like miles, crying every step. After walking, I felt tired, but I had released a lot of anger.

I would like to say to children, you are busy but should not be so busy you neglect your mother or father. Maybe they do not hear well, and that irritates you. Maybe they walk a little slower. You did too when you were small. They did not abandon you. You can be a little more attentive. You only have them for a short while.

I would like to address the absence of brothers and sisters in a widow's life. You don't call anymore; you don't invite them to visit. These are your loved ones. If you are so busy with friends you do not have time for family, you need to take another look at your own life. Everyone will go through this pain and grief. I hope you will have the love and support you need when your time comes. It's lonely out there.

I was saddened after calling several large churches in the Atlanta area to see what they offer in the way of a widow's ministry and found they have none. A gentleman answered the phone at one church and told me they did not have anything like that for widows. He said children should take care of their parents. They should give them the things they need.

I could not help but reply to the gentleman, "The Bible says to honor your father and mother. The Bible also says to the church, 'Take care of the widows and orphans.'"

Widows have told me, "It's not about things, it's about the loneliness and someone to listen." Children are not in an environment like they used to be. Parents are running to baseball, football games, and practice for their kids and do not have time for their parents. This is why they have "a place for mom."

The widows and widowers need the church and the ministry to help these individuals. The gentleman said he and his wife had discussed this type of ministry, but never did anything. At this point, he said my call was destiny. He would look into starting something. A church of twelve thousand has a lot of lost, lonely people. There are probably three to four hundred in his church alone. I hope he was serious and does something to make it happen. I intend to check back later.

You can die from a broken heart. It is a real medical condition. Some feel like they are having a heart attack, even go to the ER. This is exactly what you should do if the pain continues. One friend told me he was going home one Sunday after eating at his club house. He missed his wife; he started crying. He read somewhere to just cry it out. So he did, but then he could not stop crying. He drove into his garage and walked into his house, still crying. He sat on the couch, his heart beating rapidly, and he started to hyperventilate. Finally he called an EMT he knew, and with his help, he slowly began to calm down. He decided he could not allow this to happen again.

The Mayo Clinic recognizes the broken heart syndrome experience. Some of the symptoms include chest pains and thinking the patient is having a heart attack. They are having a disruption of their hearts' normal pumping functions in one area of the heart. The remainder of the heart functions normally or with more forceful contractions. This condition is called stress cardiomyopathy by doctors. It is treatable, and the condition usually reverses itself in a day or two.

Any symptoms with chest pains or shortness of breath should not be taken lightly. If it lasts even a short period of time, the individual should call 911 or go directly to their doctor.

The percentage of widows dying just months after their loss is high. Many widows are already in bad physical shape from the responsibility of being a caregiver. They are in a high level of stress, and their immune system is low. It is so important for the widowed to get help with caregiving, eating right, and getting plenty of rest and they should see their doctor for a physical. No one told me how bad this could be, but I do remember how it hurt. Now I understand my feelings are and were normal.

CHAPTER 14

Finding the Way Home

*Which of us has known his brother? Which of us
Has looked into his father's heart? Which of us has
not remained forever prison-pent? Which of us is not
forever a stranger and alone?*

—Thomas Wolfe

Writing this book has been a healing for me, and I hope for those who are reading my journey and the journey of others. If you are reading this and are not a widow or widower, you will be someday. As you read some of these stories, you will discover there is not a rule book for those who have lost a spouse, because every path and journey is different for each of us. I wish I had read a book like this before my loss, but then again, how could I have known I would need to? We were a couple and never imagined this happening. We were healthy, happy, and so much in love. You think you will go at the same time, but this never happens unless you are in an accident together. Even then, one usually lives.

I have met so many people who even after three years are still grieving their loss. Just when you think you have it under control, here it comes again. It is just as one widower said, "Like a big wave rolling over you."

Rachel said, "I miss Papa. I wanted him to see me graduate from high school. He left too early. I need to talk to him about what I should do." This started my wave again, accompanied with quiet tears. I have tried to keep busy teaching art to fill my days. Sometimes I am so tired at the end of the day, I can't think. But moments like these with my granddaughters Sarah and Rachael, I know I'm not the only one still hurting.

Sarah brought the waves to my mind when she had a bad tire which wouldn't hold air. She was at college and totally stressed. She said Papa had told her to go get air in it, come see him, and he would take it to get it fixed when her own father refused to help. Cliff got out of his sick bed, with objections from me, and took her car to be repaired. He filled it with gas with a little extra love for her. When we discuss Cliff, it is always about his patience, gentleness, and his giving heart, and what a great listener he was. All of what he was has been embedded in our hearts.

I have never taken a sleeping pill or one for depression. A long walk and lots of praying seems to work for me. The exercising helps me sleep better and keeps my body healthy and tired. Keeping busy doing things for others is the best medication. We don't always feel like helping someone, but it helps you. Self-pity can creep up on you.

When I start feeling depressed, my dog seems to sense it and lets me know it's time for her walk. My dog missed my husband so much, she would not eat for weeks, just lay quietly. She always slept in her dog bed during the night.

One night, I invited her to rest on my bed. She came close to me and seemed comforted. It wasn't long before she became Bella again. If she hears Cliff's name, she will bark and run to the door. I have learned that even animals grieve and don't forget. She has been a big comfort to me. She keeps me walking when I don't want to walk. Animals are medicine too.

In my interviews, I have encountered individuals struggling with questions such as, What kind of God would take my wife/husband? I prayed and prayed for their healing. What kind of God would leave me with children without a spouse to help me? How can I take my children to church and tell them to believe in God who we are told will answer our prayers when it didn't work for me?

I don't know the answers to these questions. I don't know why some die young, while others live long lives. Some people say, "God wanted another angel in heaven." The reasons people give go on and on. Why does God allow other unpleasant things in our lives and good things for people we think are evil? When we say someone died before their time, we assume everyone has an unwritten promise of a long life. The Bible doesn't make guarantees. Psalm 90:12 says, "So teach us to number our days, that we may gain a heart of wisdom." Does this mean to count our days? No, it means to make the best of our time. Don't waste one day. Love those who are left, tell them often.

Janis's long journey from depression back to life again took a strange path after her husband died. She had a desire to run away. The stress of losing her husband and her best friend was more than she thought she could handle. Most of us have said we wanted to run away at some point in our lives. Well, Janis did. After the funeral and one week of trying to cope, she bought a one-way ticket to England. She and her husband loved the countryside and had visited England often.

There were no familiar faces, no one she had to talk to. She roamed the countryside and read books to clear her mind of the loss. She and her husband had no children. She had been adopted, and there were no siblings. His parents had passed away several years earlier. The loneliness was constant. She only went by bicycle to the grocery.

There was a local church she passed every day on her walks, but she never went in. One day she saw the door open and decided to look in. She saw an elderly lady in a pew. Janis slipped in and sat behind her. The lady was weeping. This was the first feeling Janis had for someone else in eight months. She wanted to get up and go over and hug her. The lady must have felt her presence and turned around. She got up and went to Janis and asked if she needed her prayers. This gesture sent Janis into tears. She had not cried for months. She hugged the little lady and said, "Yes, please." This started a friendship greatly needed by Janis for her healing. Now she cries often, but it is for all the good memories. Janis is back home again, but has promised her new friend she will return to England.

I would like to tell you to avoid trying to talk someone out of their hurt. They have to go through this stage in the beginning. A person can try to cover the hurt, but it will come at some time. The problem is most people do not want to hear about the hurting. It makes them uncomfortable. They do not know what to say. So they wind up saying things like "Pull yourself together," or "You have to look at the future." The person is still grieving and just needs someone to listen. Let the individual cry. They have had the worst thing happen to them they will probably ever have.

The first art class I taught after Cliff's death was a numb-minding day for me. My students kept saying, "What a strong-willed person you are. You have really recovered well." With those comments, I really had to put my happy face on, even though I was hurting so bad inside. I took a lot of breaks during the class to pull myself together, to appear strong.

One of the hardest things to get used to is dining alone in a restaurant. One thing that irritates me is when the hostess asks, "How many?" When I reply one, her reply will be, "Just one?" Invariably she will seat me in the far corner. It is depressing to hear, and you will get treated differently. The world seems to be created for couples.

I accidently met a widow friend of mine on the streets of Avalon one morning. It had been two years since her loss. She did not look the same. Her hair was cut short, and she had no makeup on. I could not believe how she had let herself go. She said, "I'm sorry for the way I look, but I don't care anymore."

When we parted, I thought, even though we have lost our spouse, the world does not expect us to look like we have died too. We should look our best if we are to survive. I put my makeup on even if I am alone, and try to dress the best I can, just for me. I am starting to laugh again and care about myself more. It is so hard in the beginning when you've lost the one who told you how good that dress looked on you. But now? I just do it for me.

I have invited my friend to lunch, and hope I can help her in some gentle way. Friends can lift you, encourage you, and inspire you to look better, laugh, and get back to your old self. I am hoping I can do that for her.

Widowhood is a worldwide problem. There are an estimated two hundred and eighty-five million widows worldwide. One hundred and fifteen million live in poverty. Some have physical abuse from family members. Many are hungry and abandoned. The number of widows comes to one-seventh of the world's population. This is one of the most underreported human rights issues facing the world today. Widows seem to be at the bottom for human concern. The loss of one's spouse is painful enough, but to also experience being blamed, mistreated, abandoned, and in poverty makes it even more unbearable.

The United Nations issued a report in 2001 in which it stated, "There is no one affected more by the sin of omission than widows. They are ignored for women's poverty, human health, and human rights." Most women are linked to their husband's social status, and when he dies, she no longer belongs anywhere in that group. If widows were gathered in one geographic location, they would be the fourth largest nation in the world.

Widow's Day was organized by an international organization to raise awareness of the problems of widows. This organization adopted June 23 as the international Widow's Day. They called for other organizations to give special attention to the trials and tribulations of widows all over the world.

Here in America, we do have resources to take care of our widows, if only we would do it. Our communities do not kill widows or physically remove them from their home like some cultures do. But pain is pain and grief is grief in any language.

Bonnie and Cliff on Boat

There are one hundred and three scriptures in the Bible about widows. God commands us to care for widows and orphans. When he gave the law to Moses and the Israelites, he gave instructions for how to treat orphans and widows, along with harsh consequences promised if they failed in their responsibility. Caring for those in distress is not optional. In the Bible, Paul talks about the family taking care of the widow, and if they will not, the church should.

Generations ago, the family took the responsibility for grandmother, but in today's society this seldom happens. Children are too busy, other members of the family have their own life with schedules which leave no time for a widow. Couples do not include them because they are no longer one of them. So the question is, do we just get put at the bottom and have to stay there? I say *no*! We are a powerful force both economically and politically.

We may have changed a lot, but we can be strong and productive again with our "widow power!" We are a large group of women. We have learned how to take the journey and survive. This makes us very special. God said it, and I believe it!

I talked to a small-town southern preacher. He had a great story. Sometimes when opportunities are not open to a person, they make their own. The minister's father, who was a retired pastor, died after a lengthy illness. His mother, knowing other widows in their church, sought out two of them for support. Before long they added two more to their little group. Getting together became a weekly event. Every Monday the group would meet at someone's house. Each lady brought a dish. They ate well and started playing Rook. They began to take small trips together. This escalated to overnight excursions. Finally, they took journeys to New York and to the western states. Sometimes they drove themselves, and other times they hired a driver. At night in the hotel room, they played Rook and had a good time being together. This group lasted for many years, until members began to die or went into nursing homes.

You don't have to wait and complain there is nothing out there for widows. Sometimes you have to decide what you need and want and you make it happen.

One pastor of a small church said there are a number of widows in his church but only two widowers, he being one of them. He said the other widower was sitting home alone one night when his phone rang. A widow, who lived in the community, said she was lonely and needed someone to talk to. He replied he was lonely also, and he would come over. They have been friends since that night.

This pastor said there is another lady in his church who lost her husband three years ago, and comes every day in the morning at the same time to drink coffee with him. Sometimes she brings donuts and other times ham and biscuits. There is nothing romantically involved. They just enjoy talking to each other. Romance does not always have to be involved. Many times it is the company—someone to listen and be listened to.

I have found many churches in Atlanta which have not found a way to communicate with the widows in their church, and they do not have a widow's ministry to help with the staggering number of new widows every year.

Being widowed is a singular kind of displacement, entirely different from any other kind of separation, because it is permanent. No one really understands except for another widow. When you get a divorce, your family is not a family, but you move on. The moment a woman is at her most vulnerable, she must make choices which will have an enduring impact on her well-being.

After talking to numerous widows, churches, and organizations, I have discovered what it takes to start a ministry for widows. First, speak with church leaders or the pastor. See if they agree with your idea and are willing to help. Next, do some kind of survey to ascertain how many widows are in the church. Many may have already left. Approximately fifty percent of widows leave their church after their loss. Find out from your survey what widows in your church want and need.

When you start to organize, find a widow or widower who is willing to lead the group. This person has suffered a loss and knows how people in the group will feel. He/she can lead with compassion. Finally, take all your requests to the church, such as rooms to meet in, kitchen privileges, use of the church van or bus, and perhaps funds for guest speakers and materials.

There is a group called Grief Share that has an outlined program to begin a grief ministry which the church can purchase. It is a very popular program many churches have used.

The main thing: don't get overwhelmed; open the doors, and they will come. Opening this special place will help with uniting hearts and healing crushed spirits. It will be a group that understands if you start to cry; they understand because each one of them has had a loss. The group will share ideas for hope and survival and how to start over again.

Widows on the whole are separated from about seventy-five percent of their friendships. Even their church overlooks them and, as a result, underserves them. With help from widow's groups, we can become more confident and make our journey with purpose. We can help others as we progress. We start to look at each day with more compassion.

With help from our new group, we are encouraged to count our blessings one by one. We have not laughed much during this painful journey, but the new group laughs with us. Our new ministry group is all about making a big change. We will go one step at a time together. We now have the love of our new friends, and we can have the support to go forward.

We will be a powerful force. Widows in the US will inherit seventy percent of the fourteen-trillion-dollar wealth transfer expected over the next forty years. Widows today control forty-eight percent of estates worth over five million dollars. Widows give much to charitable organizations. Let's use this power!

After hearing the stories of grief from the loss of a spouse or divorce, I am now convinced the direction for our life depends on us. We must take time to plan out our journey, even though we are still grieving. You will always have the loss. It will cause you to pick a different path, if you want to or not.

Judy, the lady I met in Taos, New Mexico, decided to keep her eyes on the path of self-reliance. She looked for her direction from her faith in God, and He gave it to her. I have found in the lives of others we can have joy and peace going through the dark places if we only look forward instead of always looking back. When Lot's wife turned to look back at what she had lost, she became a pillar of salt. When we lose a spouse, we become a new creation, almost like being born again.

Finding our place in this strange, new world is very difficult. Divorced people go through some of the same trials by not being accepted in their old groups. There is life after pain and grief. My trip to New Mexico was a breath of fresh air. I have to admit it took me several days to get my problems out of my head and relax, putting all my stress behind. We all need to take time for "me." It helps us see things more clearly.

The widow's ministry should become faith-filled, because all need help to face another day. I could not have made my first step without it.

Many widows have had the experience while preparing dinner—she sets the table for two and, even without thinking, prepares dinner for two. When she looks at the empty chair, she realizes what she has done. The big wave rolls over her, almost suffocating her. Her tears flow. He is not coming home from work. She goes into her bedroom and prepares for bed to escape the reality of her life. Will this never end? She finds herself commenting on a TV program, looks over at the empty chair, and thinks she is losing her mind. Then a miracle happens in her life. A friend calls and invites her to a new grief ministry group starting at her church. At first she doesn't not want to be with all those strangers. Within a few minutes, she realizes she is with fellow travelers with losses like her own, and they feel and act like she does. Then the sun begins to shine in her life again.

One widow told me this story: "I could not even comb my hair for days or eat. I hardly wanted to bathe. I had one friend who would come and pray with me and just sit quietly. She held me when I cried, and after a few weeks she took me to a widow's group. My first time there, I just sat and cried. Everyone cried with me. The second time, I had more control and just talked. I have come so far, and now I am one of the leaders of the group. If it was not for this ministry, I don't think I would have survived. I discovered I was not alone."

Men and women deal with loss differently. Therefore, who are we to judge how long a person should wait? When is it too soon for a person who has suffered the worst loss of their life to find happiness and companionship again? The old saying, "Women mourn, men replace" may be true. If a man was happy in his marriage, he wants to be happy again.

Men have a higher incidence of mental and physical illness after losing a spouse than women. They also die sooner. Women may feel deserted or abandoned. Men may feel like they have lost something which kept their lives in an organized state. Women seem to be able to go on and accept grief better. Men may look for another woman for companionship. Men have fewer support networks.

There is no timeline for falling in love. No one should have guilt feelings for needing someone in their life. One friend said, "Just look at it this way: The second time around, you've got all the kinks out." It's like buying a house or car. You buy as is!

The law of attraction suggests if you feel you are worthy, you will send a message you are important. If you do the opposite, you send out a different message that you are unworthy of friendship. Then you may eat too much, dress sloppy, stop exercising, and treat others with disrespect. If you are spending your energy and time on thoughts of fear, worry, sadness, and guilt, you are losing out on a chance to connect with others.

The more you give of yourself, the more you open the door for the good light of life to pour in. Once you start interacting with people again, you will notice miraculous things happening in your everyday life.

Many people think old age is a scene of sorrow, illness, and impoverishment. Everyone wants to live a long time but no one wants to be old. Old age often comes as a surprise. It catches us unaware. We need to look at old age as a problem only we can solve. Take steps to increase your enjoyment. If you are lucky, you will have the same friends as before and do the kinds of things you have enjoyed in the past. If not, find new friends and discover different things you like to do. The flip side of this coin is boredom and depression.

There are many organizations open to you no matter your age. You don't necessarily have to seek out grief groups. While it may be good to express your grief verbally to others, this will only go so far. Get out of the house and seek new activities. Think what brings you joy. It will be different than what your neighbors enjoy. Churches offer all kinds of activities other than sitting in a pew on Sunday mornings.

As I mentioned, most community colleges offer tuition-free courses for those older individuals. You can take a college course just for the fun of it. If you choose, you can take it for credit or noncredit. If you take it for noncredit, you do not have to take tests, and you will not receive a grade. You can learn something new just for the fun of it.

Many people living alone say they have more time to do things but can't find things to do. There is little to be said for just killing time. When you start gardening, taking up painting, or just keeping a pet, you meet others with similar interests. Try calling old friends you have not heard from in years.

There are some common threads I've discovered writing this book and including these real stories from real people. One is any reaching out is not in vain. A simple touch on the arm, or a card, note, or phone call can make a world of difference.

If you have enjoyed a relationship of deep love and respect, this alone is very comforting. The length of time for mourning has nothing to do with the depth of love felt for the deceased. Each person's grief time is unique to them. Time will not make the pain of loss go away, but it will lessen the hurt. Remember, grief will take as long as it takes. When it comes down to it, there is no right or wrong way to grieve, just your way. You know you will never be the same again, which is true, but you can be happy again.

CPSIA information can be obtained
at www.ICGtesting.com
Printed in the USA
LVHW061211281019
635540LV00006B/166/P